# Protect, Backup and Clean Your PC for Seniors

# Studio Visual Steps

# Protect, Backup and Clean Your PC for Seniors

*Stay Safe When Using the Internet and Email*
*and Keep Your PC in Good Condition!*

*www.visualsteps.com*

This book has been written using the Visual Steps™ method.
Cover design by Studio Willemien Haagsma bNO

© 2015 Visual Steps
Author: Studio Visual Steps

First printing: January 2015
ISBN 978 90 5905 400 4

**Resources used**: Some of the computer terms and definitions seen here in this book have been taken from descriptions found online at the Windows Help and Support website.

**Do you have questions or suggestions?**
**E-mail: info@visualsteps.com**

**Would you like more information?**
**www.visualsteps.com**

**Website for this book:**
**www.visualsteps.com/protectpc**

**Subscribe to the free Visual Steps Newsletter:**
**www.visualsteps.com/newsletter**

# Table of Contents

# Foreword

It is very important to safeguard your computer and protect your privacy while surfing the Internet. What can you do to prevent cybercriminals from getting hold of your personal data? How do you safely use the Internet without contracting viruses on your computer? How do you make sure it is safe to shop online or do your Internet banking? It would be awful to find out that your personal data has been hijacked, or that your bank account has been emptied!

In this book we explain how to protect your computer from viruses and spyware. We also discuss some of the measures you can take when browsing the Internet or sending and receiving email.

It is also very important that you create regular backups of your computer. A backup copy will protect you from losing your valuable personal files and photos in case your computer crashes. The last topic in this step-by-step book is maintenance. We will show you how you can clean up your computer by deleting unneeded programs and files, and checking your hard disk for errors. This helps to make your computer function faster and also more efficiently.

In short, this comprehensive title is indispensable for any computer user that values good security measures, privacy, and a well-functioning computer!

The Studio Visual Steps authors

P.S.
When you have completed this book, you will know how to send an email. Your comments and suggestions are most welcome.
Our email address is: mail@visualsteps.com

# Visual Steps Newsletter

All Visual Steps books follow the same methodology: clear and concise step-by-step instructions with screenshots to demonstrate each task.
A complete list of all our books can be found on our website **www.visualsteps.com**
You can also sign up to receive our **free Visual Steps Newsletter**.
In this Newsletter you will receive periodic information by email regarding:
- the latest titles and previously released books;
- special offers, supplemental chapters, tips and free informative booklets.
Also, our Newsletter subscribers may download any of the documents listed on the web page **www.visualsteps.com/info_downloads**

When you subscribe to our Newsletter you can be assured that we will never use your email address for any purpose other than sending you the information as previously described. We will not share this address with any third-party. Each Newsletter also contains a one-click link to unsubscribe.

# Introduction to Visual Steps™

The Visual Steps handbooks and manuals are the best instructional materials available for learning how to work with the computer. Nowhere else can you find better support for getting to know your PC or *Mac*, your iPad or iPhone, Samsung Galaxy Tab, the Internet and a variety of computer applications.

Properties of the Visual Steps books:
- **Comprehensible contents**
  Addresses the needs of the beginner or intermediate user for a manual written in simple, straight-forward English.
- **Clear structure**
  Precise, easy to follow instructions. The material is broken down into small enough segments to allow for easy absorption.
- **Screenshots of every step**
  Quickly compare what you see on your screen with the screenshots in the book. Pointers and tips guide you when new windows or alert boxes are opened so you always know what to do next.
- **Get started right away**
  All you have to do is turn on your computer or laptop and have your book at hand. Perform each operation as indicated on your own device.
- **Layout**
  The text is printed in a large size font and is clearly legible.

In short, I believe these manuals will be excellent guides for you.

dr. H. van der Meij
Faculty of Applied Education, Department of Instructional Technology, University of Twente, the Netherlands

# What You Will Need

To be able to work through this book, you will need a number of things:

The primary requirement for working with this book is having the US or English version of *Windows 8.1* or *Windows 7* installed on your computer or laptop. *Windows* comes equipped with all the programs you need to work with this book.
**Please note:** The screenshots shown in this book have been made using a local user account. It is also possible to login with a *Microsoft* account. Since this is a book for beginning computer users, we have chosen to not to use this type of account. If you are working with a *Microsoft* account, you will sometimes see different windows and other options.

In order to download *Microsoft Security Essentials* and some programs you will need an active Internet connection.

# Prior Computer Experience

If you want to use this book, you will need some basic computer skills. If you do not have these skills, it is a good idea to read one of the following books first:

**Windows 8.1 for SENIORS** - ISBN 978 90 5905 118 8
**Windows 7 for SENIORS** - ISBN 978 90 5905 126 3

# How To Use This Book

This book has been written using the Visual Steps™ method. The method is simple: just place the book next to your computer or laptop and execute all the tasks step by step, directly on your own device. With the clear instructions and the multitude of screenshots, you will always know exactly what to do. This is the quickest way to become familiar with *Windows 8.1* and use the various programs and services it offers.

In this Visual Steps™ book, you will see various icons. This is what they mean:

**Techniques**
These icons indicate an action to be carried out:

 The mouse icon means you need to do something with the mouse.

The keyboard icon means you should type something on your keyboard.

 The hand icon means you should do something else, for example, turn on the computer or carry out a task previously learned.

In addition to these icons, in some areas of this book extra assistance is provided to help you successfully work through each chapter.

## Help
These icons indicate that extra help is available:

 The arrow icon warns you about something.

 The bandage icon will help you if something has gone wrong.

1 Have you forgotten how to do something? The number next to the footsteps tells you where to look it up at the end of the book in the appendix *How Do I Do That Again?*

In this book you will also find a lot of general information and tips. This information is displayed in separate boxes.

## Extra information
Information boxes are denoted by these icons:

 The book icon gives you extra background information that you can read at your convenience. This extra information is not necessary for working through the book.

 The light bulb icon indicates an extra tip for using a program or service.

# The Website Accompanying This Book

On the website that accompanies this book, **www.visualsteps.com/protectpc**, you will find additional information about this book.
Please, take a look at our website **www.visualsteps.com** from time to time to read about new books and gather other useful information.

# Test Your Knowledge

Accompanied with some Visual Steps books, you can test your knowledge online on the **www.ccforseniors.com** website. By answering a number of multiple choice questions you will be able to test your knowledge of the Mac. If you pass the test, you can also receive a free *Computer Certificate* by email, if you wish. Participating in the test is **free of charge**. The computer certificate website is a free service from Visual Steps.

# For Teachers

This book is designed as a self-study guide. It is also well suited for use in a group or a classroom setting. For this purpose, we offer a free teacher's manual containing information about how to prepare for the course (including didactic teaching methods) and testing materials. You can download the teacher's manual (PDF file) from the website which accompanies this book: **www.visualsteps.com/protectpc**

# The Screenshots

The screenshots used in this book indicate which button, folder, file or hyperlink you need to click on your computer screen. In the instruction text (in **bold** letters) you will see a small image of the item you need to click. The line will point you to the right place on your screen.
The small screenshots that are printed in this book are not meant to be completely legible all the time. This is not necessary, as you will see these images on your own computer screen in real size and fully legible.

On the next page you will see an example of an instruction text and a screenshot. The line indicates where to find this item on your own computer screen.

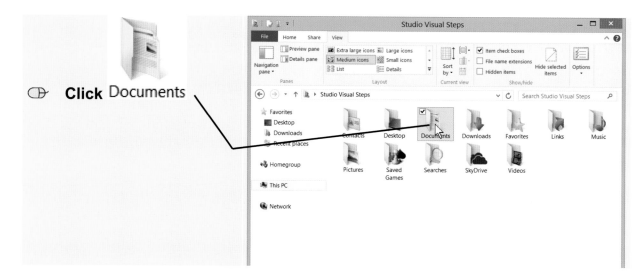

Sometimes the screenshot shows only a portion of a window. Here is an example:

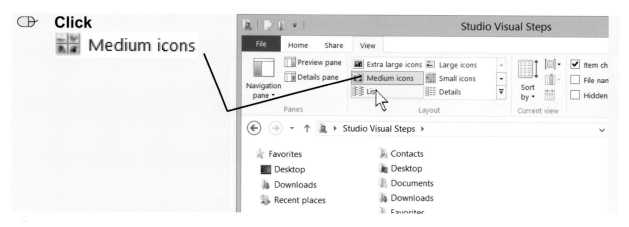

It really will **not be necessary** for you to read all the information in the screenshots in this book. Always use the screenshots in combination with the image you see on your own computer screen.

# 1. Protecting Your Computer

It is essential that your computer is protected when it is connected to the Internet. Adequate security measures will reduce the risk of your computer becoming infected by *malware* (viruses or any other type of harmful software).

It can be very frustrating if your computer becomes infected by viruses. Not just for you, but for others too. If your computer has been infected, it can also infect other computers. This can happen without you even noticing it, when you send an email or share files, for example.

As a computer user, you are responsible for protecting your own computer. Above all, it is important that you keep your *Windows* version *updated* and all other programs that are used on a regular basis as well. This means that a new, enhanced version of the program will be installed. Updating will also solve any recent security problems.

*Windows 8.1* will help you protect your computer with the *Windows Defender* program. *Windows 7* uses *Microsoft Security Essentials* for protection. Another security tool offered by *Windows* is the *Action Center*. In the *Action Center* you can check the security settings for the *Windows* version on your computer and adjust them, if necessary. You can also check to see if *Windows Firewall* has been enabled. This is a protective service that will eliminate unwanted access from others.

It is also important that you enable the security options for your Internet browser programs, such as *Internet Explorer*. This will prevent *phishing websites* from making attacks, among other things. A p*hishing website* will often display false information in order to obtain important personal data, such as the access codes for your Internet banking services.

*Add-ons*, also called *plugins*, add extra functionality to an Internet browser. Usually they work quite well, but they can also cause problems. That is why it is useful for you to learn how to manage your add-ons.

In this chapter you will learn:

- what malware is;
- how to update *Windows*;
- how to update other software programs;
- more about antivirus software;

- how to work with the *Action Center*;
- how to work with *Windows Defender* in *Windows 8.1*;
- how to work with *Microsoft Security Essentials* in *Windows 7*;
- how to use *Windows Firewall*;
- what phishing is;
- how to enable the anti-phishing options in an Internet browser;
- how to enable other security options in an Internet browser;
- how to work with add-ons or plugins in Internet browsers.

# 1.1 What is Malware?

The term *malware* is a contraction of *malicious software*, in other words, dangerous or harmful software. It is a generic term for all kinds of software that can damage your computer.

Some of these programs are built by persons who enjoy breaking into other people's computers (this is called *hacking*), or who want to distribute annoying programs. But nowadays, an increasing number of professional criminals are exploiting the speed, convenience and anonymity of the Internet to commit a wide range of criminal activities. *Cybercrime,* another name for this type of illegal activity, can be very profitable and generate millions of dollars for criminal organizations.

There are different types of malware:

- *Virus* is a generic term for small programs that can be executed independently but which are attached to another program. Once the infected program is opened, the virus is automatically activated. Some of these viruses will not do a lot of damage. For example, they might display a certain message on your screen on a certain date, but nothing else. Other more aggressive viruses will take up more and more space on your hard drive and infect ever more programs, and in the end you will no longer be able to use your computer. A common characteristic of these viruses is the ability to multiply, making it easier for them to spread out on their own. For instance, by sending one to the people in your address book through an email message.

- *Worms* and *Trojan horses* (or *Trojans*) are different kinds of viruses. These programs can be just as harmful as viruses, but they function independently and have no connection to other programs. They are often used by computer hackers who want to take over your computer in order to use it for criminal activities, such as breaking into large company websites.

- *Spyware* is not a virus, but harmful software that is secretly copied to your computer when you install an infected program or visit a harmful website. Spyware is used to spy and collect data stored on your computer and pass it on to dishonest organizations or criminals. They will use this data to send you unwanted emails containing advertisements (spam), for example.

- *Adware* will insert advertisements into your window while you are surfing, or open additional popup windows in your Internet browser. Adware often appears after downloading and installing a program that was available for free.

- In the last few years, a new type of virus called *ransomware* has appeared. This software is actually malware, and it can cripple your computer. You may receive a message, telling you that you can 'retrieve' your computer by transferring a certain amount of money. Another version of this type of ransomware will send you a message, informing you that you have conducted illegal business with your computer (allegedly), and that you can prevent the police from arresting you by paying a certain sum of money. You should never react to this kind of blackmail and it should be reported to the police immediately.

## 1.2 Updating Windows

*Windows* is continuously being enhanced and improved. The additions and improvements are distributed by *Microsoft*, by way of so-called *software updates*. These may be minor updates with just a few changes. But they can also be major updates, called *Service Packs*.
It is important to install these *Windows* updates as soon as possible. They can sometimes contain critical patches to close security holes and prevent your computer from being hacked or infected with viruses.

The *Windows* software updates are installed by the *Windows Update* utility. This is a tool that checks whether you are using the most recent version of *Windows*. Usually *Windows Update* is set to automatically update, but you should check this setting yourself to make sure.

You may also need to manually update *Windows* sometimes, instead of waiting for the automatic update to do its job. For example, if you notice that *Windows* is no longer functioning correctly. Sometimes, an update can solve this problem.

 **Please note:**

*Microsoft* never sends software updates by email. If you happen to receive an email that states that the attachment contains *Microsoft* software or a *Windows* update, you should never open the attached file. Delete the email immediately, and be sure to delete the email from the *Deleted items* folder as well. These types of emails may be sent by criminals that want to install harmful software on your computer.

You can open *Windows Update* from the *Control Panel*.

In *Windows 8.1*, from the Start screen:

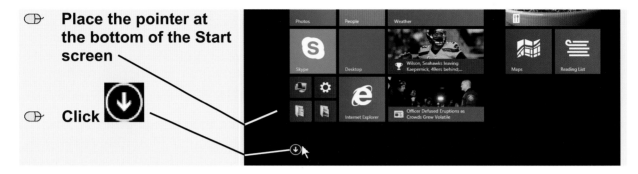

⬧  **Place the pointer at the bottom of the Start screen**

⬧  **Click** 🔽

You will see all the apps on your computer:

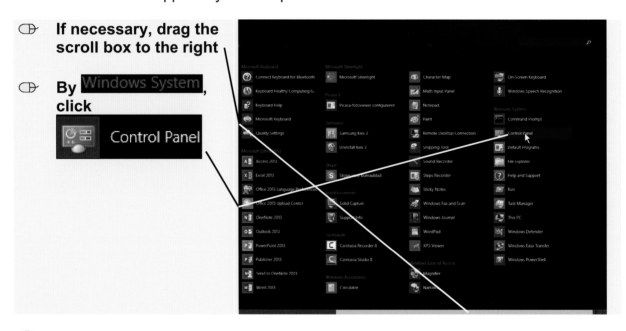

⬧  **If necessary, drag the scroll box to the right**

⬧  **By** Windows System, **click** 🖥 Control Panel

💡  **Tip**

**Control Panel in Windows 8.1**

Another way to open the *Control Panel* in *Windows 8.1* is by right-clicking the ⊞ start button on the taskbar and selecting Control Panel in the menu that appears. You can also type 'Control panel' in the Start screen.

In *Windows 7*:

⬧  **Click** 🪟, Control Panel

Next, in both versions:

◑ **Click** System and Security

◑ **Click** Windows Update

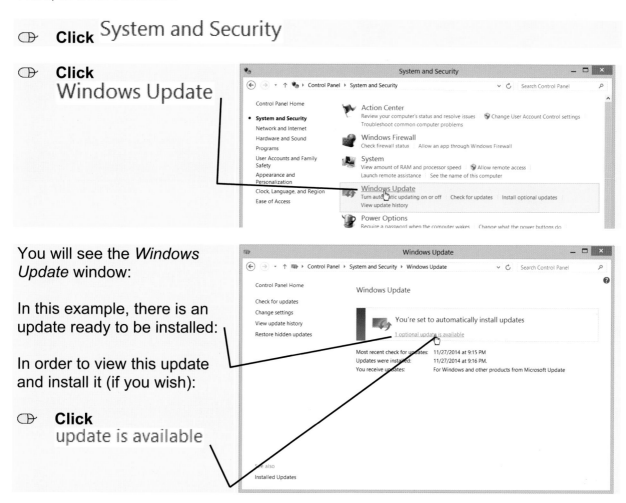

You will see the *Windows Update* window:

In this example, there is an update ready to be installed:

In order to view this update and install it (if you wish):

◑ **Click** update is available

You will see the updates that can be installed. To install an update:

◑ **Check the box** ☑ **by the desired update**

In *Windows 8.1*:

◑ **Click** Install

In *Windows 7*:

◑ **Click** OK

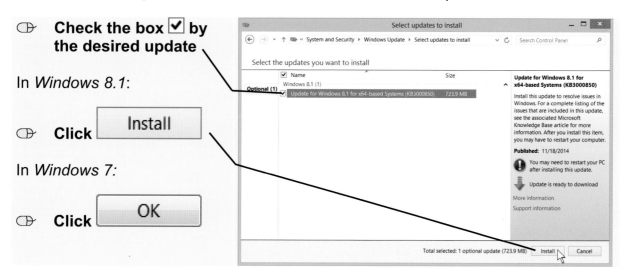

To install an update in *Windows 7*:

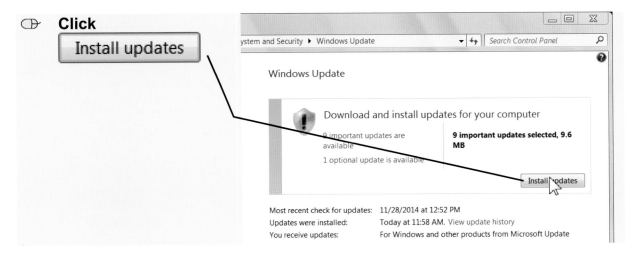

Normally, *Windows* will search for new updates all by itself and install them automatically at the designated time, or whenever you turn off your computer. But you can check for updates yourself and install them, if the need arises. For instance, if you notice that *Windows* is not functioning properly.

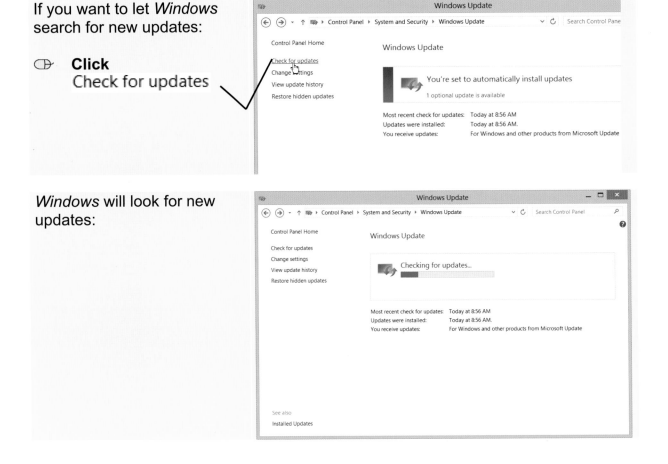

If any new updates have been found, they will appear in the window:

In order to view these updates and install them, click update is available.

Follow the steps as previously described, starting on page 19.

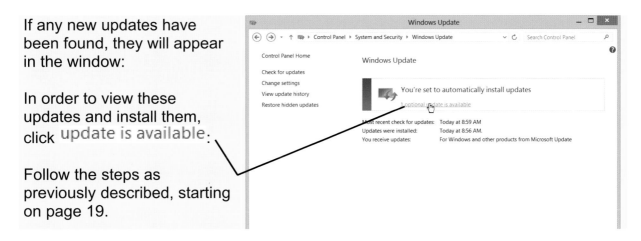

If you want to be certain you are using the most recent *Windows* version, you will need to enable the *Automatic Update* function. You can do that as follows:

☞ **Click** Change settings

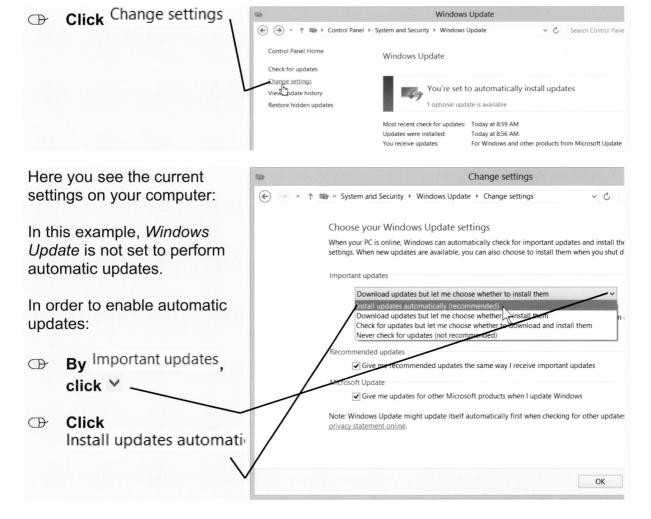

Here you see the current settings on your computer:

In this example, *Windows Update* is not set to perform automatic updates.

In order to enable automatic updates:

☞ **By** Important updates, **click** ✓

☞ **Click** Install updates automatic

In future, *Windows Update* will check for updates automatically and install them.

All you need to do now is to decide when the *Automatic Update* function should be performed. In *Windows 8.1*:

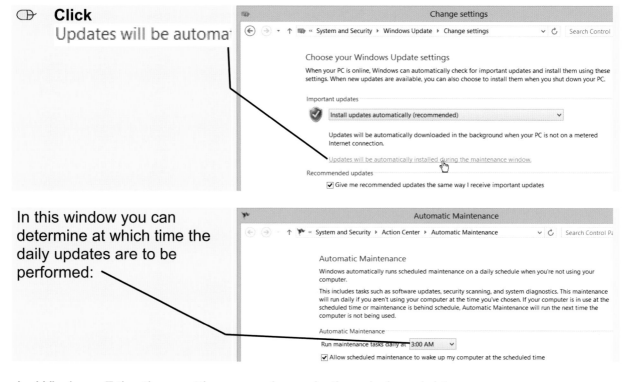

| | **Click** |
| :-- | :-- |
| | Updates will be automa |

In this window you can determine at which time the daily updates are to be performed:

In *Windows 7* the time settings are shown in the window right away.

In this example, *Automatic Updates* is set to be checked every day at 3:00 AM. If the computer is turned off at that time, the system will check for new updates as soon as the computer is turned on again. The available updates will be downloaded and installed automatically. *Windows* might display a message at the bottom of your screen, but usually you can just keep on working. In the case of a major update, it may be necessary to restart your computer.

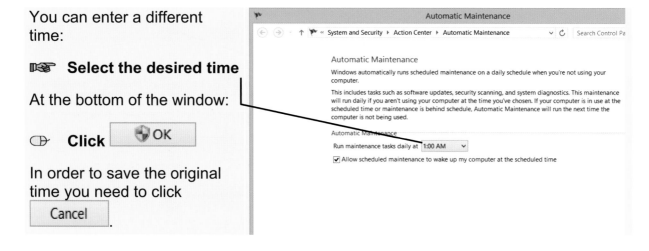

You can enter a different time:

☞ **Select the desired time**

At the bottom of the window:

**Click**  **OK**

In order to save the original time you need to click

Cancel .

If you have changed a setting:

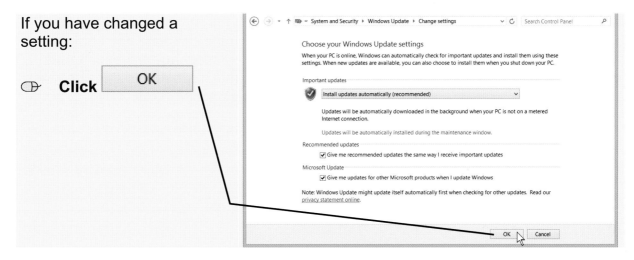

☞ **Click** OK

☞ **Close the *Control Panel*** **[1]**

💡 **Tip**

**The drawbacks of automatic updates**

One of the disadvantages of having the system check for and install updates automatically is that *Windows* may unexpectedly ask you to restart your computer at any moment. You may be engaged in activities you do not want to interrupt. You may have a program opened and were working on a particular file. A pop-up window normally appears if a restart is needed. In this window, you can select the option to have the restart postponed. But what happens if you have stepped away from your computer and are not around?

If you have left your desk for a minute and the restart was scheduled for that time (usually within ten minutes or so), then when you return, you may notice that your computer has restarted and your work has been lost (if you had not saved it).

If you want to prevent this from happening, you can change the settings and choose a convenient time for the updates to be installed. Just make sure to check if any updates need to be installed on a regular basis.

# 1.3 Updating Other Software

What goes for *Windows* also goes for other programs you frequently use: it is important to update these programs on a regular basis. Software can be vulnerable and can also pose a security threat, especially the programs that connect to the Internet such as Internet browser applications.

Apart from that, almost all computers contain 'hidden' software, such as *Java* and *Flash*. *Java* and *Flash* are mainly used to enable the connection to an interactive website. This allows you to play videos and games on certain websites, for example. It is therefore important that you use the most recent versions of *Java* and *Flash*.

Most software programs are set to update automatically. Sometimes this can go unnoticed. In other cases, you may see an onscreen message letting you know that new updates for a certain program have been found. The message will usually ask you if you want to install them. Sometimes you will be able to postpone this action for a short time. It is wise to install these updates as soon as possible. Usually this does not take very long.

Before you begin updating programs it is recommended that you save any work you are currently busy with such as writing text in a *Word* document. Make sure you also have an antivirus program installed on your computer that will block any suspicious updates that pose as legitimate software programs. You can read more about this subject in later sections of this chapter.

 **Tip**

**Updating Microsoft programs**
When a *Windows Update* is performed, many times other *Microsoft* programs on your computer are updated as well, for instance, *Internet Explorer* and *Office* programs such as *Word* and *Excel*.

 **Tip**

**Updating Internet browsers**
Along with *Internet Explorer*, other Internet browser applications are also updated on a regular basis. Usually you will receive an automatic message when you open the Internet browser in question. In that case, you need to follow the onscreen instructions in order to update the browser software.

New updates are also often displayed in the taskbar. One example of this is a *Java* software update. The following screenshot shows that there is a *Java* update available:

If a program icon is not visible in the taskbar right away:

☞ **Click** ▲

☞ **Place the pointer on the program icon**

If there is an update available, you may see a small bar containing a message:

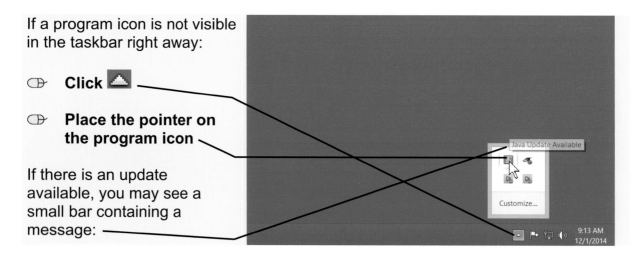

In order to install the update:

☞ **Right-click the icon**

☞ **Click** Install

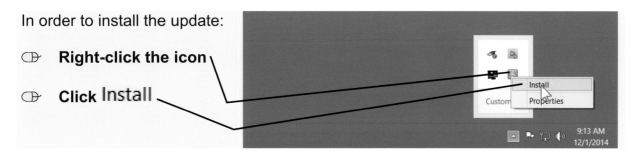

In most cases, the update will now be installed. If this does not happen, you can also start the updating procedure through the properties window of the program concerned. You can do this by opening the program first, and then clicking the properties or options windows (often indicated by the 'gear' icon). You can also open the properties window by clicking the program's icon on the taskbar:

☞ **Right-click the icon**

☞ **Click** Properties

You will see the window with the properties for this program:

Automatically check for new updates: ⎯⎯⎯⎯⎯

Date of last update: ⎯⎯⎯⎯

In order to install the latest update:

☞ **Click the update button**

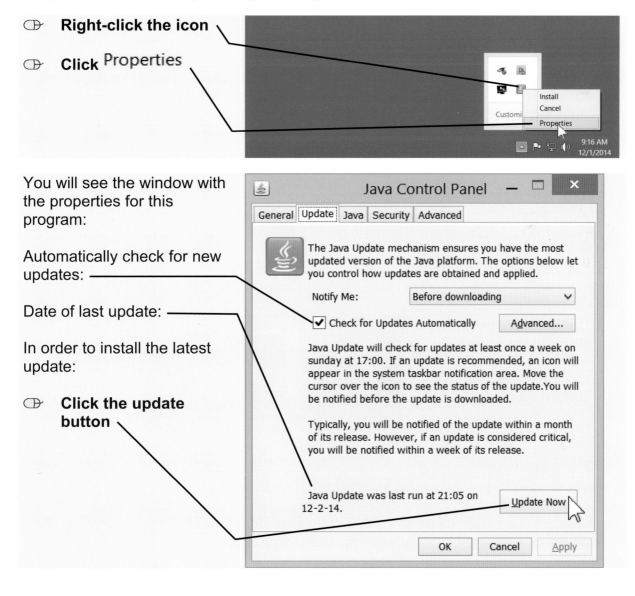

Now you will see the install window:

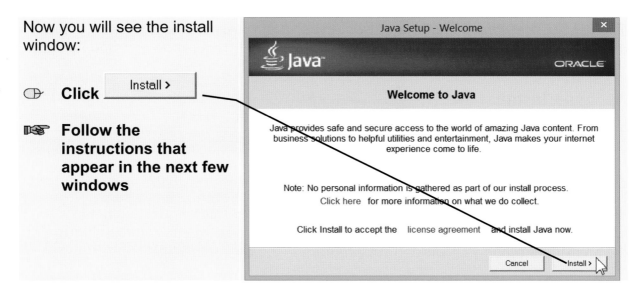

 **Click** [ Install > ]

 **Follow the instructions that appear in the next few windows**

 **Please note:**

Sometimes you will need to restart the computer after the update has been installed. You will see a message regarding this. If the window contains a button with which you can restart your computer, do not forget to save your work in other programs first, before you click this button.

💡 **Tip**

**Updating Adobe software**
Most *Adobe* programs, such as *Adobe Reader* (a program for viewing PDF files), can also be updated by clicking an icon on the taskbar.

You can often search for updates within the program itself. Usually the program menus contain a separate option for this, for example, Extra or Help:

👉 **Click the menu with the update option**

👉 **Click the update option**

 **Please note:**

You can install programs from various sources, such as a DVD or a website. If you want to install a program from a website, it is recommended to get the program from the manufacturer's website or, in case it is an app, from the *Windows Store*. There are numerous download sites where you can download programs, but not all of them are trustworthy.

The individual apps in *Windows 8.1* sometimes require an update too. Usually, these apps are different from the programs mentioned above. This is how you update apps that appear on the Start screen:

An update is indicated by a
number that appears on the
Start screen, on the *Store* tile:

You may see a different number on your own screen or there may not yet be any updates available for your apps. In this example there are fifteen available updates for various apps:

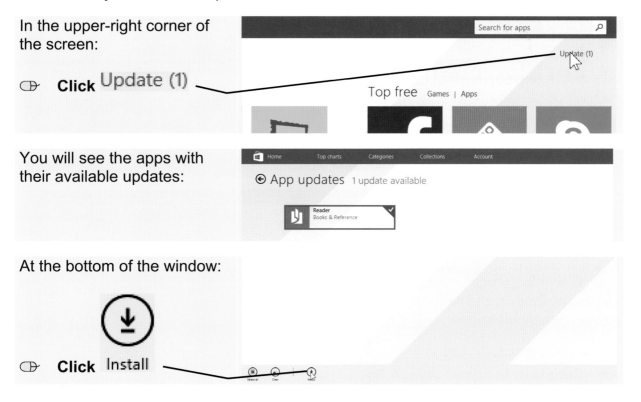

⮞ **Click** Store    1

This is how you install the updates:

In the upper-right corner of
the screen:

⮞ **Click** Update (1)

You will see the apps with
their available updates:

At the bottom of the window:

⮞ **Click** Install

The updates will be installed. You can monitor the progress of this operation:

Once the update for an app has been installed, the icon for it will disappear from the screen. After all the updates have been installed, you will see this screen:

Click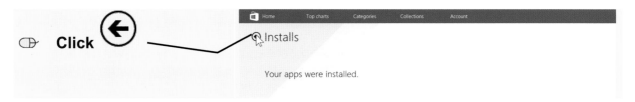

If the setting for automatic updates has not been enabled for this app, you can check to see if one is available:

**Position the pointer in the top right-hand corner of the screen**

**Click Settings**

**Click App updates**

**Click**

**Check for updates**

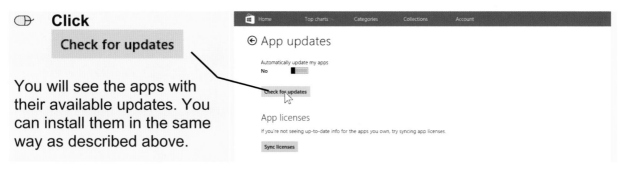

You will see the apps with their available updates. You can install them in the same way as described above.

☞ **Return to the Start screen** 👣²

# 1.4 Antivirus Software

Antivirus software, also called an antivirus scanner, is a very important part of your computer security. Antivirus software constantly monitors your computer, in order to identify harmful programs at once, and render them harmless.

If you do not have an antivirus program installed on your computer, your computer is at risk. And if the license or subscription of your current antivirus program has expired, and you cannot update the latest antivirus information, your computer is in just as much danger. You will need to purchase a new license as soon as possible, or install a new antivirus program on your computer.

There are many free and paid antivirus programs available on the market. Many paid antivirus programs offer free trial periods of thirty, sixty, or even ninety days. In this way you can try an antivirus program and see if you like it, before you buy it.

Among the good free programs we can suggest are *AVG*, *Avast!*, *Windows Defender*, and *Microsoft Security Essentials*. You need to realize that some of the free antivirus programs do not offer any support from the manufacturer (although the programs mentioned above do offer some support).

Also be aware that free programs will often contain fewer options and features than the paid versions. Viruses and spyware are detected and disabled, but extra options, such as spam filters and protection while buying online items, for example, will often be missing. Some of these free antivirus programs do not remain consistently active in the background, but will only take action if you *tell* them to check for viruses and spyware. As a result, a harmful program may be noticed too late, after it has already done some damage to your computer.

As a final thought, know that some free antivirus programs are only available for home or private use, and not for business. Also many free programs are often just free for a single year. After that, you may be bombarded with requests to migrate to the paid version.

There is another type of free option available. You can use an online service to scan your computer for malware. These online scanners are offered by well-known manufacturers of antivirus software as a means of promoting their products. These scanners do not work in the background to prevent viruses from infecting your computer. They only work from the moment you activate them. Some examples of online antivirus scanners are:

Bitdefender: www.bitdefender.com/scanner/online/free.html
Eset: www.eset.com/home/products/online-scanner
Panda: www.pandasecurity.com/homeusers/solutions/activescan

The free online antivirus scanner offered by Eset:

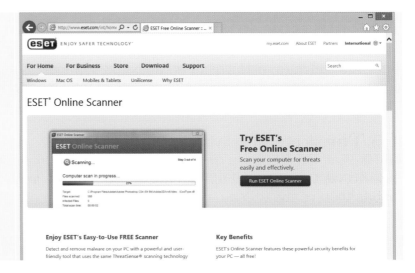

 **Please note:**

Beware of fake online antivirus scanners. Never react to offers on websites where they have allegedly found viruses on your computer and offer a free scan of your computer. The only intent of these so-called 'offers' is to install malware on your computer.

The best-known paid programs that we can recommend are *Norton/Symantec* and *McAfee*. But less well-known programs such as *G Data* or *Panda* are also good. These programs are offered in free demo/trial versions, for a period of fifteen, thirty, or sixty days. Annual subscriptions are then available from $30 and up.

You will get a year's worth of current virus updates to keep your software functioning properly. Towards the end of the year, you will be asked to renew your subscription. If you own more than one computer, it is cheaper to purchase a subscription that is good for multiple computers, so they will all be protected. This is often much cheaper than buying separate versions of the programs.

You can buy antivirus software in a store, but it is often easier and sometimes even cheaper to purchase the software directly from the manufacturer's website.

For more information, you can visit the websites from the following manufacturers:

McAfee: www.mcafee.com
Bitdefender: www.bitdefender.com
Kaspersky: www.kaspersky.com
Nod32: www.eset.com
Norton: www.norton.com
Panda: www.pandasecurity.com
G Data: www.gdatasoftware.com
Avira: www.avira.com

**Tip**

**Tests**
You can regularly read the test results and reviews of antivirus programs in computer magazines and on various websites.

# 1.5 The Action Center

The *Action Center* in *Windows* checks the security settings of your computer and keeps track of the *Windows* updates. You can also view and manage the maintenance status of your computer and solve some of your computer problems.

This is how you open the *Action Center*:

☞ **Open the *Control Panel*** ³

⊕ **Click** Review your computer's status

In the *Action Center* you can view the status of the main components that play a part in securing your computer, such as:

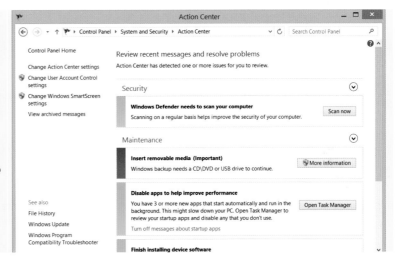

- *Firewall*
- *Automatic updates*
- *Protection against spyware and unwanted software*
- *Virus protection*
- *Other security settings*

At a glance you can see which problems your computer currently has. Problems are indicated by a red or yellow color. The red color stands for a major problem that needs to be addressed as soon as possible, for example, turning on the virus protection options. The yellow color stands for a maintenance task that can be set into action, such as updating the computer with *Windows Update*.

🦢 **Please note:**
The settings or messages on your computer may differ from the ones in this example.

☞ **Close the *Action Center*** ⑂¹

##   Tip

**Detect problems by icon changes on the taskbar**

On the taskbar, you can immediately see if there are any security or maintenance problems with your computer. If you see an icon with a flag and a red cross on the right-hand side of the taskbar, this means a problem has been identified:

☞ **Place the pointer on**

You will see a message with a brief summary of the problems:

☞ **Click**

Now you will see a separate window with a more detailed description of the problems:

You can click a link directly, in order to view a window containing tips to help solve the problem:

☞ **Click**
   **Open Action Center**

Here you see the *Action Center*:

You will see the problems at once:

☞ **Drag the scroll box downwards**

Extra options for solving the problems:

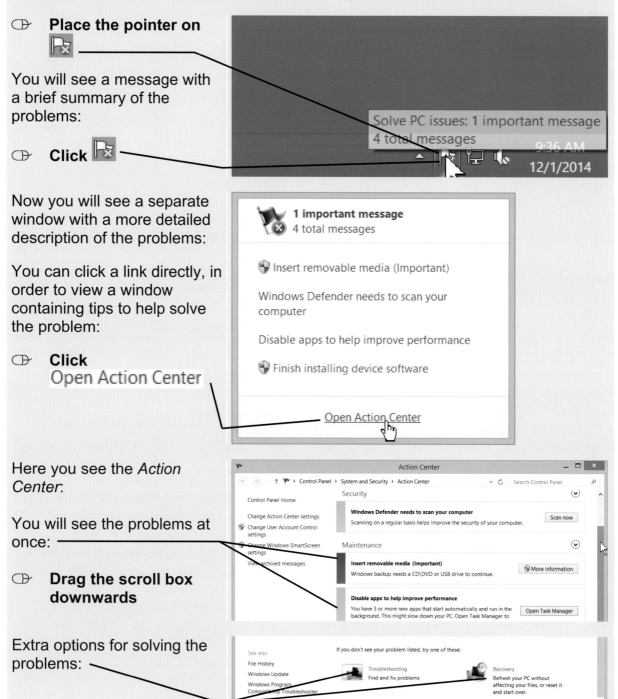

# 1.6 Windows Defender and Microsoft Security Essentials

Malware is software that has been developed to harm your computer. Viruses, worms, spyware, and Trojan horses are all types of unwanted software.
The source of an infection can be an email attachment, or a newly, downloaded program. Your computer can also get infected when you exchange data through USB sticks, CDs, DVDs, or other storage media that are infected with malware. Some malicious software can even be programmed in such a way that it is executed at unexpected moments, and not only during installation. You can read more about this in *section 1.1 What is Malware?*

*Windows Defender* is one of the built-in programs in *Window 8.1*. It will help protect your computer from harmful software. For *Windows 7*, *Microsoft Security Essentials* is available, free of charge.
Both of these programs work in a similar way as other antivirus programs. They protect your computer in two ways:

- **Real-time security**
  You will be warned when harmful software tries to install itself or is installed to your computer. You will also be warned if any program or app attempts to change important settings.
- **Scanning**
  You can scan your computer any time you want. For example, if you notice that your computer does not seem to be functioning properly, or if you have received a suspicious-looking email. In such a case, you can start a scan, to check to see if you have unintentionally downloaded any malware.

 **Please note:**

It is possible that you have a different antivirus program installed on your computer and therefore *Windows Defender* or *Microsoft Security Essentials* has been disabled. New computers are often equipped with antivirus programs that are not manufactured by *Microsoft*, and are offered for a free trial period, just to promote the program. Or perhaps you or one of your acquaintances has already installed an antivirus program. In that case, it is wise to keep using the program that has been installed previously. You just need to read through the sections about *Windows Defender* or *Microsoft Security Essentials*. If necessary, you can take a look at the manual or help screens of your current antivirus program, in order to compare the actions you need to perform on your computer.
If you are not sure if any other antivirus program has been installed, you will automatically see this when you try to open *Windows Defender* or *Microsoft Security Essentials*. This is because when a new antivirus program is installed, the existing program will be disabled by default. The reason for this is that it is unwise to use two different antivirus programs on the same computer at the same time. They may hamper each other in their tasks.

This is how you open *Windows Defender* in *Windows 8.1*:

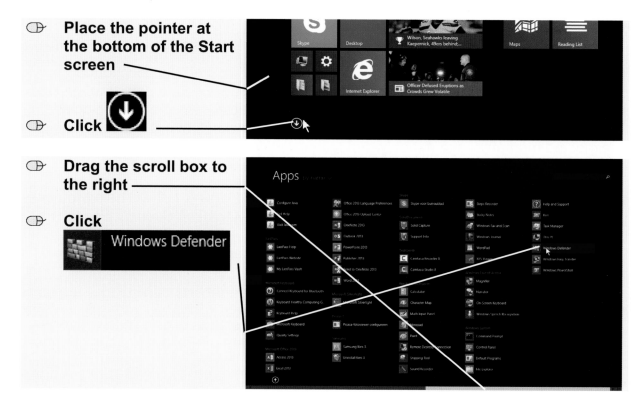

☞  **Place the pointer at the bottom of the Start screen**

☞  **Click**

☞  **Drag the scroll box to the right**

☞  **Click**  Windows Defender

The home window of *Windows Defender* appears.

This is how you open *Microsoft Security Essentials* in *Windows 7*:

☞  **Click**  , ▶  All Programs ,  Microsoft Security Essentials

**HELP! I cannot find Microsoft Security Essentials.**

If you do not see the option for opening *Microsoft Security Essentials* in the Start menu, the program has not yet been installed. You can download and install it for free. For more information, see *Appendix B Downloading Microsoft Security Essentials* at the end of this book.

## HELP! This app has been disabled.

If another antivirus program has already been installed, other than *Windows Defender* or *Microsoft Security Essentials*, you will see a warning message. In this case, you can just read through this section and carry out the actions needed for your own antivirus program later on.

Click  | Close

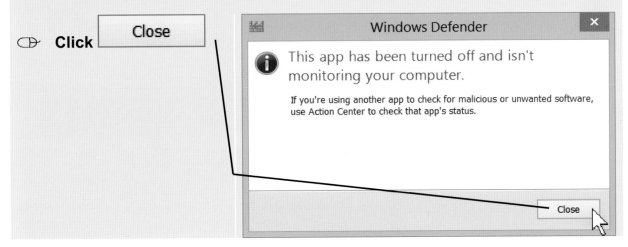

 ## Please note:

*Microsoft Security Essentials* works roughly in the same way as *Windows Defender*. That is why you can follow the same instructions.

By default, *Windows Defender* has been activated:

✅ Real-time protection: is **On**:

In this example, a quick scan has been done today:

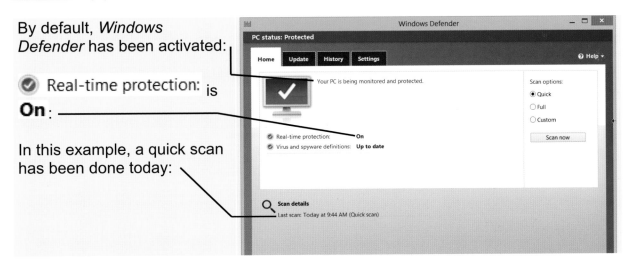

*Windows Defender* works closely together with *Windows Update*. As soon as new spyware and malware definitions (updates) are available, they are downloaded and installed automatically. This means the program always stays up-to-date. Before a scan is done, an extra check regarding the update status is performed. We encourage you to keep this default setting intact.

You can also update *Windows Defender* yourself:

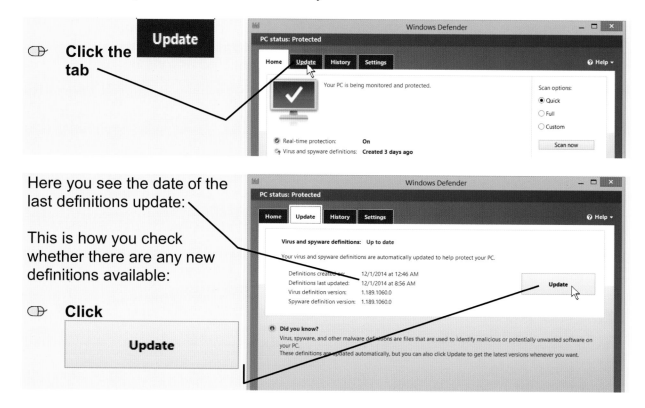

☞  **Click the tab**

Here you see the date of the last definitions update:

This is how you check whether there are any new definitions available:

☞  **Click**

**Update**

If new definitions have been found, *Windows Defender* will be updated at once:

In this example you can see the update is in progress:

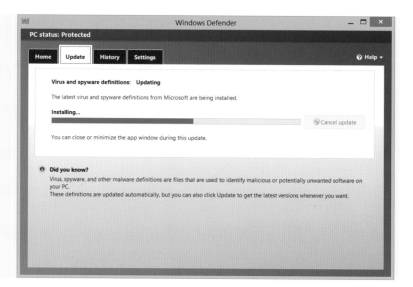

The real-time security function in *Windows Defender* will immediately warn you when it detects malware or spyware that is trying to install itself on your computer. When *Windows Defender* detects harmful software, you will see a message on your screen.

The harmful software will be moved to the quarantine location right away, in order to prevent it from being executed. You can take a look at it later on, and decide whether you want to delete or restore the item in question. You can do that as follows:

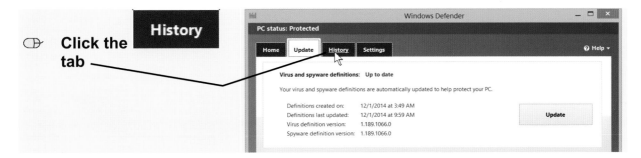

☞ **Click the** [**History**] **tab**

In *Microsoft Security Essentials* you can see right away the items that have been placed in the quarantine folder.

In *Windows Defender* you do not see these items right away. To view them:

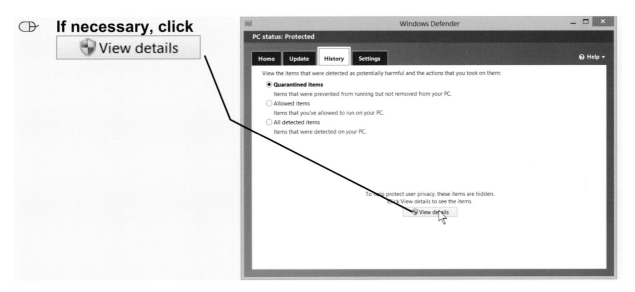

☞ **If necessary, click** [🛡 **View details**]

You may need to give permission to continue:

👉 **If necessary, give permission to continue**

You will see a summary of the items that have automatically been placed in quarantine. You can read more about quarantine further on in this section. The list on your own computer may be empty.

If the list contains an item that you know not to be harmful, you can check the box ☑ by this item and use the **Restore** button to restore it:

This is how you delete everything:

☞ **Click** **Remove all**

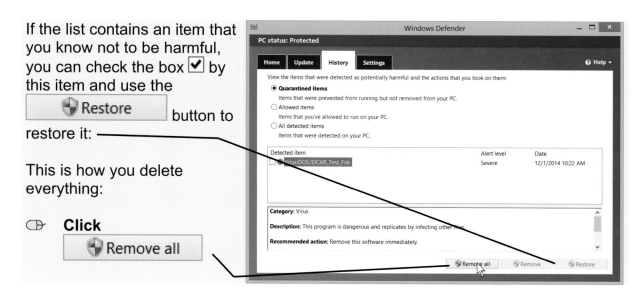

All harmful software has been deleted.

You can scan your computer with *Windows Defender* at any given moment. For example, when you feel your computer is not working properly, or if you have received a suspicious-looking email. If you want to make sure that your computer has not been infected by a virus or other kinds of malicious software, you can do a scan.

You can choose between three types of scans:

- **Quick**: only scans the locations where unwanted software is often found.
- **Full**: scans all the files and folders on your computer.
- **Custom**: only scans the folders you have selected (see the *Tip* at the end of this chapter).

To get an idea of how a scan works, you can do a quick scan.

☞ **If necessary, click the Home tab**

☞ **If necessary, click the radio button ◉ by Quick**

☞ **Click** **Scan now**

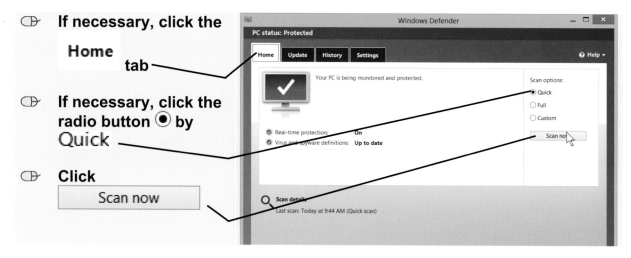

The scan will start right away, and you will see its progress:

If you want to stop the scan, you can click the Cancel scan button:

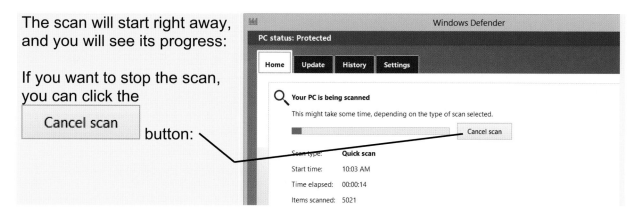

A full scan may take a few minutes but it can also take up to an hour or more: this depends on the speed of your computer and on the number of files. The quick scan is much faster. While the scan is in progress, you can continue working on the computer.

Once the scan has finished, you will see a scan report.

In this example, no suspicious files have been found:

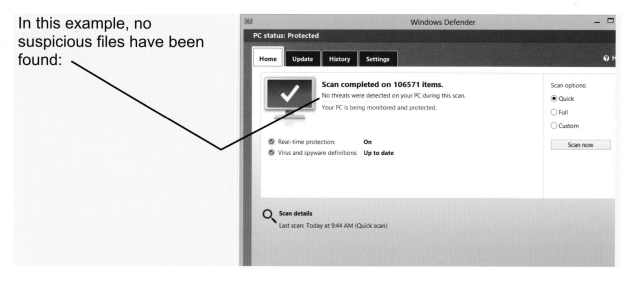

If you do not open any unknown email attachments, or use any dubious programs, there is less chance of your computer being infected by a virus. Nevertheless, *Windows Defender* may still find a suspicious file every now and then.

If anything is found, you will see a message. You will see a description of the harmful software, an indication of how serious the threat is, and what action *Windows Defender* recommends you to take.

There are several options if this occurs:

- **Remove**: the infected file or virus will be deleted from your computer. This means that the file's content will be lost if you have not created a backup copy. This is usually done of there is no other solution for the problem.
- **Quarantine**: the item is placed in a folder where it can do no damage. If you find you need this file later on, you can restore the item. Select this option if you are not sure that the item is harmful.
- **Allow**: in future scans, this item will no longer be tagged. Select this option only if you are sure the item is safe and you want to keep it.

If there are no suspicious files found on your computer, you can just read through the next section.

If a suspicious file has been found, you will see this message:

You can view the details:

☞ **Click** Show details

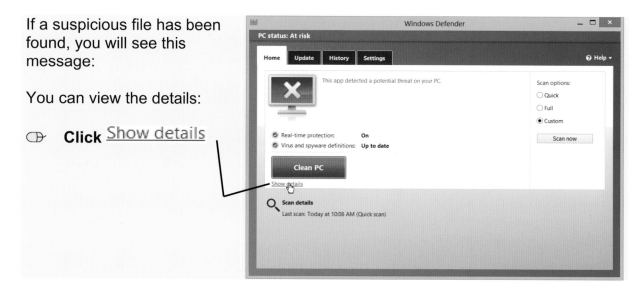

*Windows Defender* recommends to **Remove** the file:

You can do that as follows:

☞ **Click** Apply actions

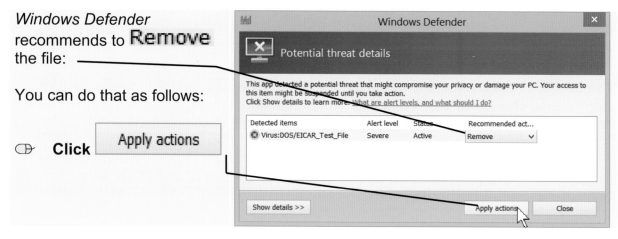

The file will be removed from the computer. You can close the window:

 **Click**

You have now become acquainted with a number of options in the *Windows Defender* or *Microsoft Security Essentials* program. You can close the program:

☞ **Close *Windows Defender* or *Microsoft Security Essentials* ৪৪¹**

 **Tip**

**Create regular backups**
Your computer contains files that are important to you: precious photos, important emails from family and friends, legal documents, favorite website addresses, and contact information. This is why it is essential that you create a backup of these files. You can read more about creating backups in *Chapter 3 Creating Backups.*

**Tip**

**Deleting persistent malware**
You can delete most malware with an antivirus program, but sometimes a harmful program will still remain active on your computer. A portion of the software can remain stored on your computer even after the antivirus program has removed the program. This portion may be able to infect your computer all over again. There is also a type of malware that inhibits the functions of an antivirus program, and may even prevent new malware definitions from being updated.

If this has happened to your computer, you will need to use a program that is designed specifically for the removal of a certain malware. This type of program is offered by the manufacturers of antivirus software.
You can look for this type of program on the antivirus software manufacturers' websites, or search for one on google.com. You can use the name of the malware detected by your antivirus program and enter this name as a keyword.

*- Continue on the next page -*

If you want to delete the malware that is detected by using a special program, you usually need to follow an extensive procedure. This procedure can be found on the web page of the virus removal software. Make sure to follow the instructions very carefully, step by step, because if you do not do this, there is a chance that the malware will not be not completely deleted and it could infect your computer again. If you are not an experienced computer user, you should ask a more experienced user to help you.

In the very worst case, you may have to re-install all the software on your computer.

# 1.7 Using Windows Firewall

A *firewall* is a type of software that manages the incoming and outgoing data traffic between your computer and the Internet or other networks. Depending on the settings of your firewall, data traffic is blocked or access is allowed.
The word 'firewall' sounds safer than it actually is. A firewall does **not** protect your computer against viruses. If the firewall allows your email program to connect to the Internet, you may still receive an email attachment that contains a virus. The firewall does not check the contents of the data traffic.

 **Please note:**

You may have a different firewall installed on your computer. A firewall is often automatically installed along with an antivirus program.
You should not have more than one firewall installed on your computer. Having multiple firewalls can hinder the programs from working properly.

☞ **Open the *Control Panel* $\mathscr{QQ}^3$**

👆 **Click System and Security**

👆 **Click Windows Firewal**

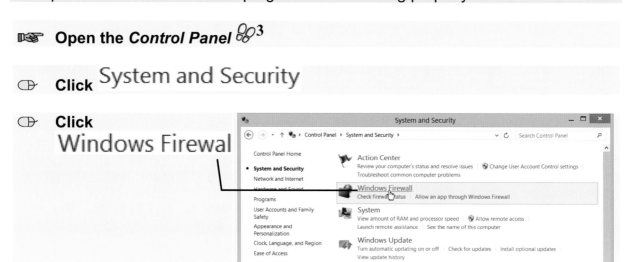

The green icon 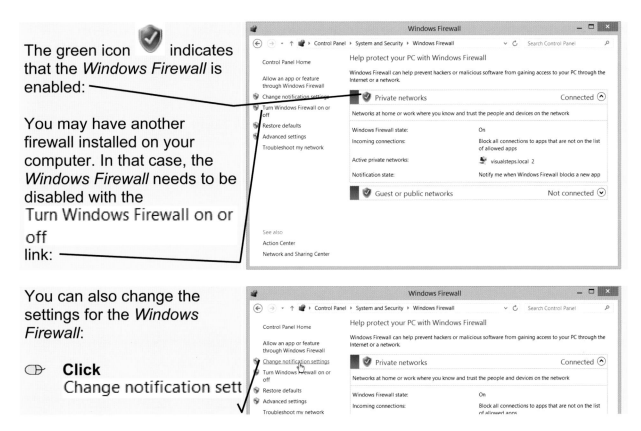 indicates that the *Windows Firewall* is enabled:

You may have another firewall installed on your computer. In that case, the *Windows Firewall* needs to be disabled with the
Turn Windows Firewall on or off
link:

You can also change the settings for the *Windows Firewall*:

☞ **Click**
Change notification sett

Your screen may turn dark and you will need to give permission to continue:

☞ **If necessary, give permission to continue**

You will see the *Customize Settings* window:

You can turn on a firewall for different types of networks:

Block all the programs, for example, in case of a wireless public network:

Send a notification when a new app or program is blocked:

In most cases, the default settings offer sufficient protection.

☞ **Click** Cancel

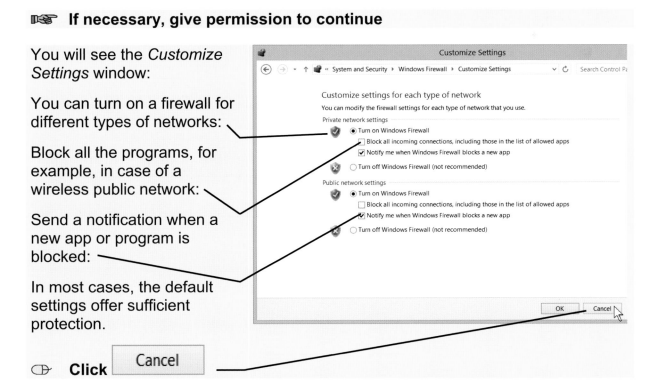

If you are using a program that needs to receive data from the Internet or from another network, the firewall will ask you to allow the connection. You can set this up in the next window:

**Click**
**Allow an app or feature through Windows Firewall**
**or**
**Allow a program or feature through Windows Firewall**

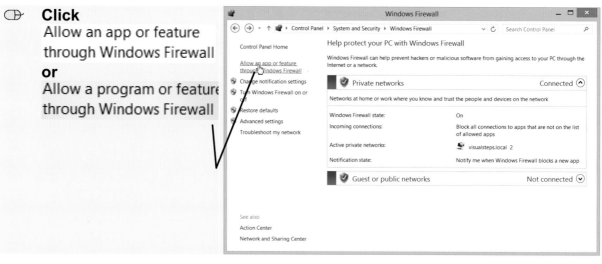

For each connection that is allowed, an exception is added to this list:

You can use the *Change settings* or *Allow another program* buttons to add exceptions:

For now you do not need to change these settings:

**Click**    Cancel

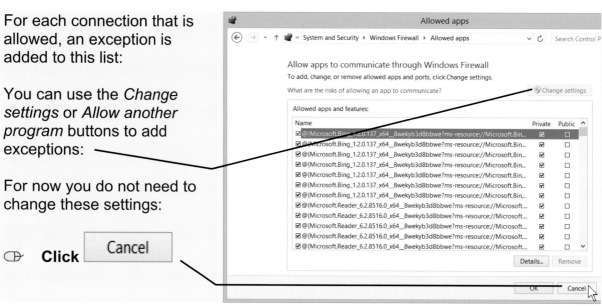

☞ **Close the** *Control Panel* ⏍¹

# 1.8 What is phishing?

*Phishing* is a method of persuading unsuspecting computer users to disclose their personal data or financial information by posing as a legitimate person or organization. In fact, phishing is a way of 'fishing' for information.

A familiar tactic in phishing is to send a fake email message that looks like a real message sent by a familiar, trusted source. This might be your bank, credit card company, a web store, or another website you have previously visited. These fake messages are sent to thousands of email addresses.

In the email, the recipients are asked to check their bank data, for instance. The message contains a hyperlink for this purpose. If the link is clicked it may lead you to a website that may look like a bank's website. There you will be asked to enter personal information, such as name and address, bank account numbers, and PIN codes, supposedly to check if everything is OK.

An example of a phishing mail:

This mail asks the clients from this bank to enter their personal information on a certain website. Criminals can then gain access to these accounts and empty them out.

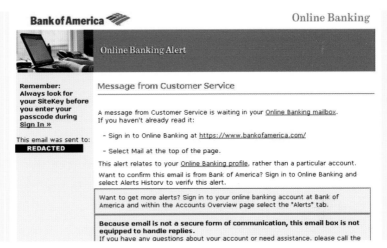

If you fall for this trick and enter your data, the information will be sent immediately to the criminals who have set the trap. Next, they may use your data to purchase items, open new credit card accounts in your name, or abuse your identity in other ways. These phishing mails and websites have a deceptively genuine look. They often use the bank's logo in the email, and the website may look like the legitimate website.

In *Internet Explorer*, the *SmartScreen filter* helps you detect phishing websites. The SmartScreen filter uses three methods to protect you from phishing expeditions:

- It compares the address of the website you visit to a list of websites that *Microsoft* has reported to be trustworthy.
- It analyses the websites you have visited, in order to find out if they have any characteristics that are similar to those of other known phishing websites.
- On request of the user, it lets *Microsoft* check whether a specific web address is mentioned in the most recent list of phishing websites.

If the website you are visiting is listed in the list of reported phishing websites, *Internet Explorer* will display a warning page and a message. On this warning page you can continue surfing, or close the page. If the website displays the characteristics of a phishing website, but is not on the list, *Internet Explorer* will insert a remark in the address bar about this website possibly being a phishing website. This is how you open the options for the SmartScreen filter:

☞ **Open *Internet Explorer* ꝏ⁴**

⊕ **Click** ⚙

⊕ **Click** Safety

You will see the options for the SmartScreen filter:

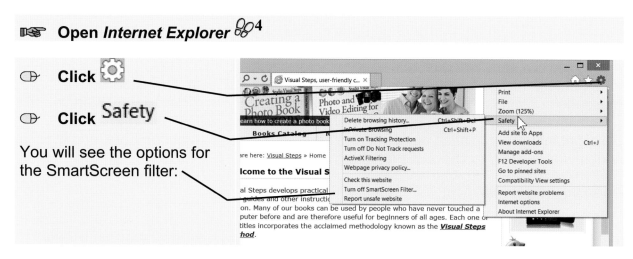

- Check this website: if you are visiting a website you do not trust, you can use this option to check if the website is included in the *Microsoft* list.
- Turn off SmartScreen Filter…: if you select this option, the website you are visiting will no longer be checked. We advise against using this option.
- Report unsafe website: if a website is not reported as a suspicious website or a phishing website, and you think it is a fraudulent website, you can report this website to *Microsoft*.

When you report an untrustworthy website, you will see a form:

Here you can indicate whether you think it is a phishing website or if the website contains malware:

Here you select the website's language:

In order to prevent automated reactions, you need to type the characters you see here: ───────

When you have completed the form:

 **Click** Submit

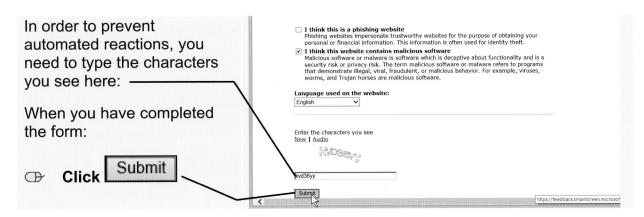

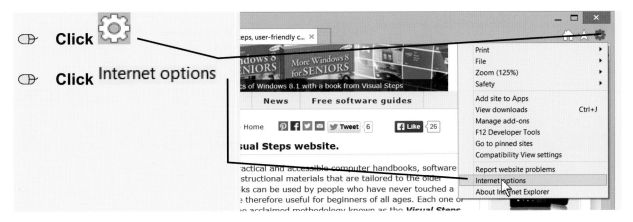 **Please note:**

The SmartScreen filter warns you about the majority of phishing websites, but is does not provide 100% security. If a website has not yet been reported to *Microsoft* as a phishing website, you will not get a warning. This is why you should be on the alert yourself.

Other popular Internet browsers, such as *Mozilla Firefox* and *Google Chrome*, have anti-phishing options too. These can be found among the other security and privacy settings. You can read more about these options in the next section.

# 1.9 Security Settings in Internet Browsers

In *Internet Explorer* you can select a security level for accessing the Internet. In this way you can determine how *Internet Explorer* should react to different websites.

To view the security settings:

**Click** ⚙ ───────

**Click** Internet options

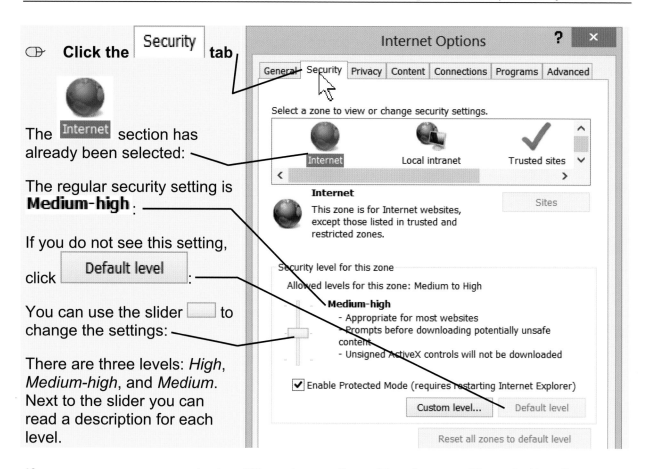

Click the **Security** tab

The **Internet** section has already been selected:

The regular security setting is **Medium-high**.

If you do not see this setting, click **Default level**:

You can use the slider ▢ to change the settings:

There are three levels: *High*, *Medium-high*, and *Medium*. Next to the slider you can read a description for each level.

If necessary, you can select a different security setting for specific websites that you do or do not trust. Take a look at the trusted websites option:

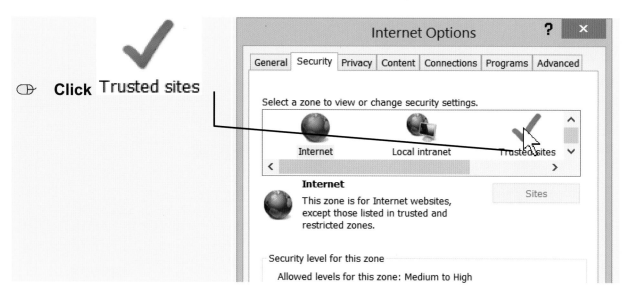

Click **Trusted sites**

You will see that the security level for trusted websites is **Medium**:

You can use the slider again to change your settings.
You can choose between five levels: *High*, *Medium-high*, *Medium*, *Medium-low*, and *Low*.

The *Low* setting is only intended for the websites you trust completely.

To add a website to the trusted websites:

☞ **Click** | Sites |

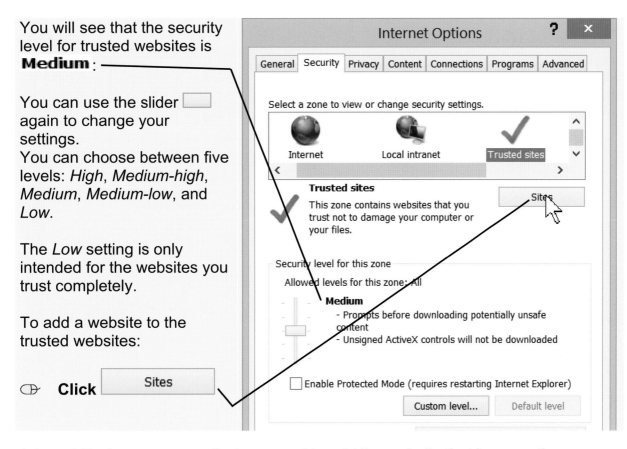

*Internet Explorer* assumes that you want to add the website that is currently displayed to the trusted websites, and has already copied the web address into the field. You can add another website, for example, your bank's website:

⌨ **Type the web address of your bank in the field, by**
**Add this website to t**
**for example**
`https://www.`
`bankofamerica.com`

☞ **Click** | Add |

The list on your computer may already contain a few trusted websites.

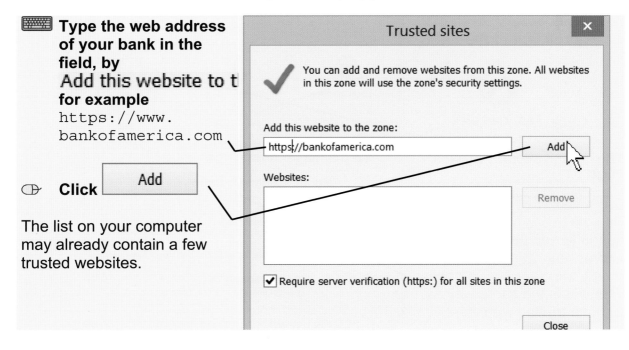

## Please note:

The setting Require server verification (https:) for all sites in this zone means that the websites you add to the trusted websites, all need to have the prefix https://. This prefix indicates that your connection is secured. The information that is exchanged between this website and your computer is encrypted and cannot be read by others.

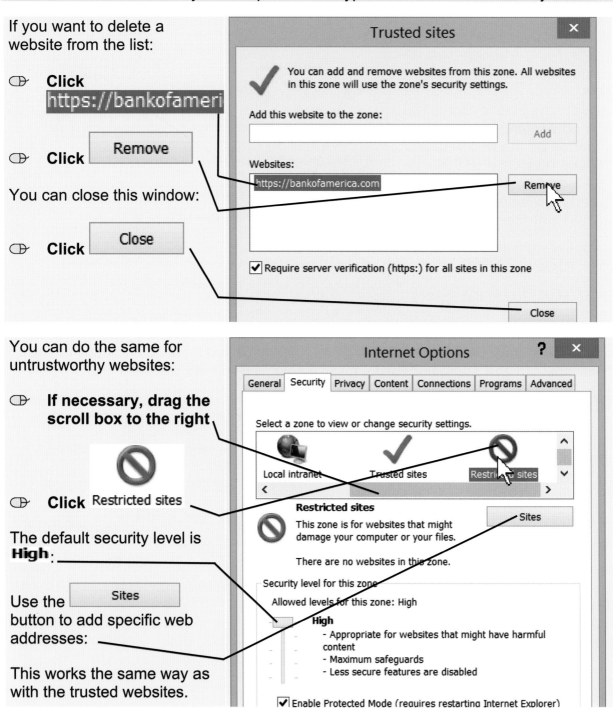

If you want to delete a website from the list:

☞ **Click** https://bankofameri

☞ **Click** Remove

You can close this window:

☞ **Click** Close

You can do the same for untrustworthy websites:

☞ **If necessary, drag the scroll box to the right**

☞ **Click** Restricted sites

The default security level is **High**:

Use the Sites button to add specific web addresses:

This works the same way as with the trusted websites.

Do you use the *Internet Explorer* app in *Windows 8.1*? The settings you change here will also be transferred to the *Internet Explorer* app.

If you want to apply a change:

☞ **Click** OK

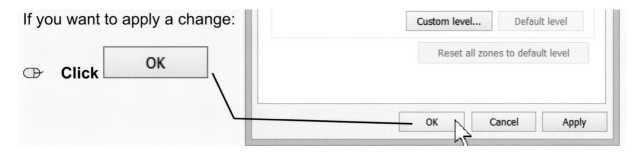

☞ **Close** *Internet Explorer* 𝄢¹

Other popular Internet browsers, such as *Mozilla Firefox* and *Google Chrome*, also offer a variety of security options.

This is how you display the security options in *Mozilla Firefox*:

☞ **Open** *Mozilla Firefox*, **if you wish** 𝄢⁵

If the menu bar is not visible:

☞ **Right-click a blank section next to the tab**

☞ **Click** Menu Bar

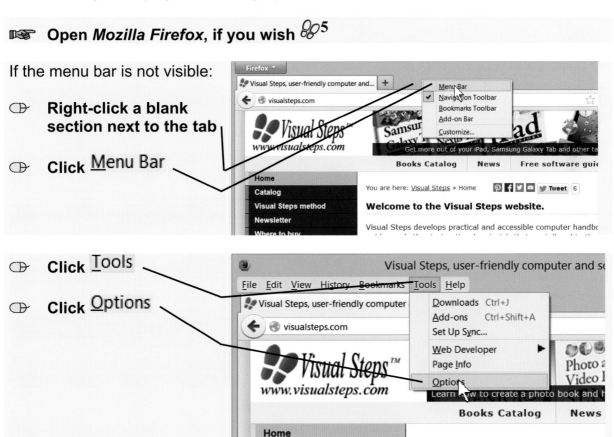

☞ **Click** Tools

☞ **Click** Options

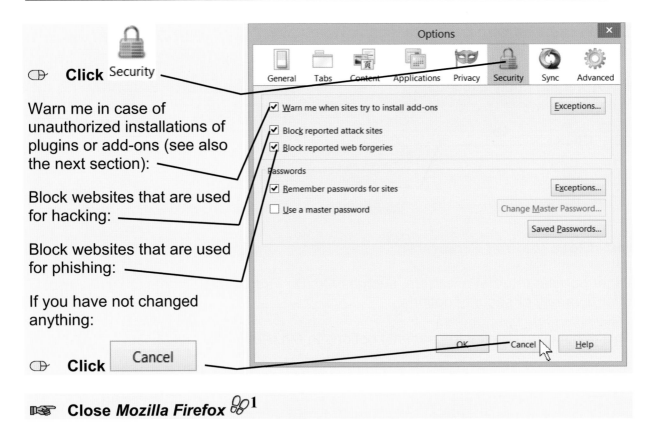

☞ **Click** Security

Warn me in case of unauthorized installations of plugins or add-ons (see also the next section): ─

Block websites that are used for hacking: ─

Block websites that are used for phishing: ─

If you have not changed anything:

☞ **Click** Cancel

📖 **Close** *Mozilla Firefox* 👣¹

This is how you display the security settings in *Google Chrome*:

📖 **Open** *Google Chrome*, **if you wish** 👣⁶

☞ **Click** ≡

☞ **Click** Settings

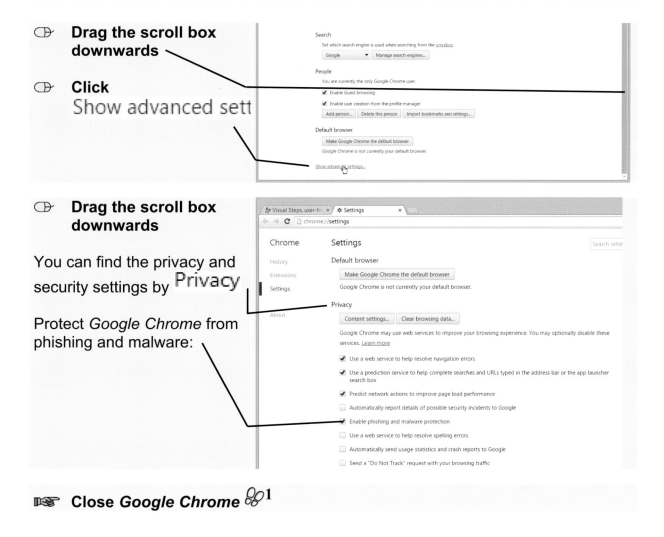

☞ **Drag the scroll box downwards**

☞ **Click**
Show advanced sett

☞ **Drag the scroll box downwards**

You can find the privacy and security settings by Privacy

Protect *Google Chrome* from phishing and malware:

☞ **Close** *Google Chrome* ℘¹

# 1.10 Working with Add-Ons

An *add-on* is a program that adds extra functionality to a web browser, such as the *Internet Explorer* browser. Examples of add-ons are extra toolbars, special pointers, and pop-up blockers. Add-ons are also known as *ActiveX controls*, *Plug-Ins*, *Extensions, Browser Extensions*, or *Browser Helper Objects*.

You can acquire add-ons very easily from the Internet. Most of these add-ons require your permission to download them to your computer. But some add-ons may be downloaded without you even noticing it. This may happen if the add-ons are included in a program you have recently installed. Some add-ons are installed with the installation of *Windows 8.1*.

Usually, you can use an add-on without worrying about it. But sometimes, an add-on will cause *Internet Explorer* to shut down unexpectedly. This can happen if the add-on has been developed for a different version of *Internet Explorer*.

This is how you view the add-ons that have been installed for *Internet Explorer*:

☞ **Open *Internet Explorer* ⅋4**

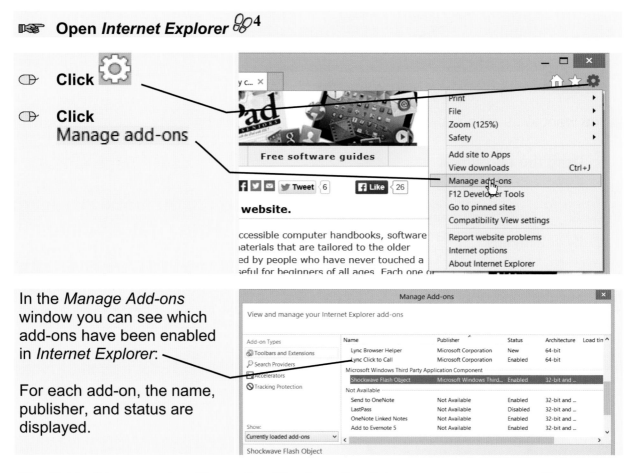

⊕ **Click** ⚙

⊕ **Click Manage add-ons**

In the *Manage Add-ons* window you can see which add-ons have been enabled in *Internet Explorer*:

For each add-on, the name, publisher, and status are displayed.

The list in this example will usually differ from the list on your own screen. If you do not use or trust an add-on, you can disable it:

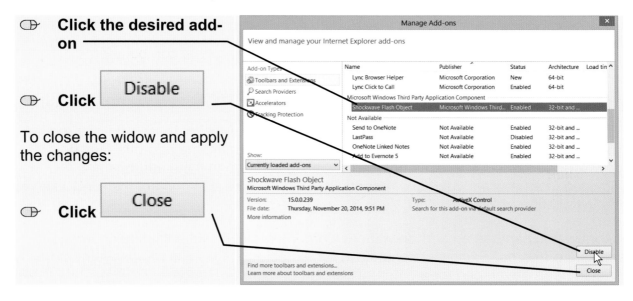

⊕ **Click the desired add-on**

⊕ **Click** Disable

To close the widow and apply the changes:

⊕ **Click** Close

To make sure that these changes to your browser have been made, you need to close and re-open *Internet Explorer*:

☞ **Close** *Internet Explorer* ℗¹

☞ **Open** *Internet Explorer* ℗⁴

If you want to use the add-on after all, you can re-enable it:

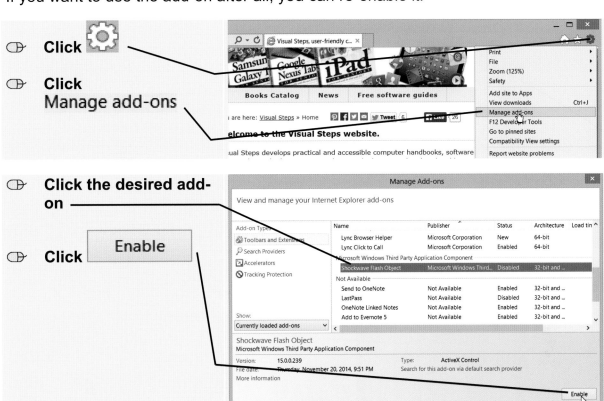

Before you close the window, you can view other add-ons that can be used in *Internet Explorer*:

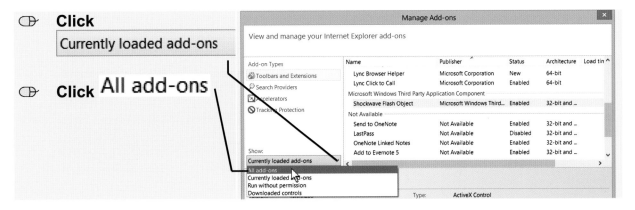

Now you will see the full list of add-ons available for *Internet Explorer*.

The list in this example will probably differ from the list in your own window.

You do not need to change anything in this window:

⊕ **Click** Close

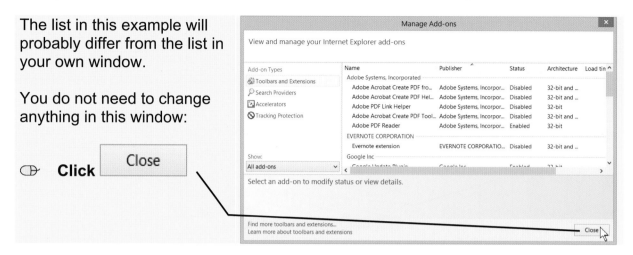

☞ **Close** *Internet Explorer* 📖¹

In the *Mozilla Firefox* Internet browser you can add various add-ons too. These are called add-ons and plugins in *Mozilla Firefox*. This is how you display the add-ons:

☞ **Open** *Mozilla Firefox* 📖⁵

☞ **If necessary, display the menu bar** 📖⁷

⊕ **Click** Tools

⊕ **Click** Add-ons

You will see the page with the add-ons:

By clicking 🔲 Plugins, you will see the plugins that are installed:

Plugins are a certain type of add-on.

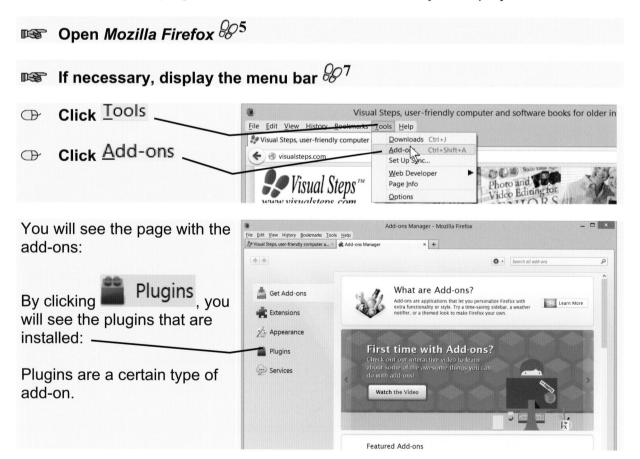

☞ **Close** *Mozilla Firefox* ᎒᎒¹

There are also various add-ons available for the *Google Chrome* Internet browser. These are called extensions in *Google Chrome*. This is how you display the add-ons:

☞ **Open** *Google Chrome* ᎒᎒⁶

⊕  **Click** ☰

⊕  **Click** More tools

⊕  **Click** Extensions

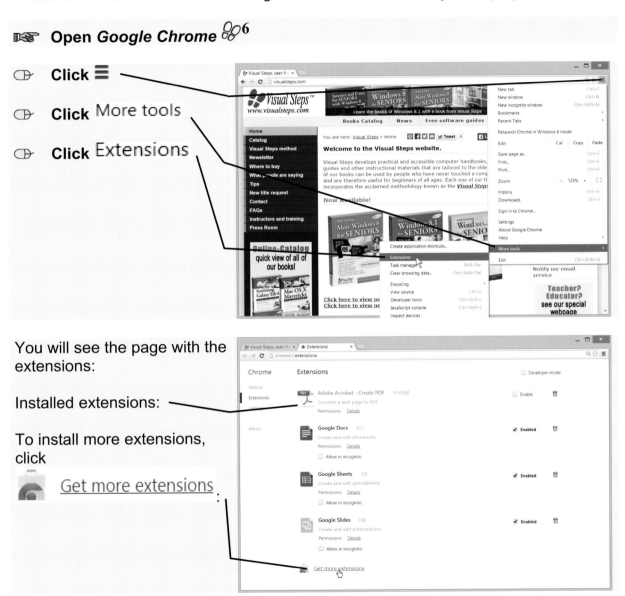

You will see the page with the extensions:

Installed extensions: —

To install more extensions, click

Get more extensions :

☞ **Close** *Google Chrome* ᎒᎒¹

In this chapter you have become aware of how important it is to update *Windows* and scan for malware on a regular basis. You have also learned about the anti-phishing and security options in your Internet browser.

# 1.11 Background Information

**Dictionary**

| | |
|---|---|
| **Action Center** | The *Action Center* in *Windows* checks your computer's security settings and keeps track of the *Windows* updates. You can also view the maintenance status of your computer in the *Action Center* and solve problems, if necessary. |
| **Add-on** | A program that adds extra functionality to an Internet browser, such as *Internet Explorer*. Also known as a plugin or an extension. |
| **Custom scan** | An option in an antivirus or antispyware program which only scans the folders that you select. |
| **Firewall** | Software or hardware that contributes to the protection of your computer. A firewall can block or allow data traffic to and from your computer. |
| **Full scan** | An option in an antivirus or antispyware program that scans *all* the files and folders on your computer. |
| **Malware** | Short for malicious software. This is software that is developed to damage your computer. Viruses, worms, spyware, and Trojan horses are types of unwanted software. |
| **Microsoft Security Essentials** | A complete solution for your Internet security in *Windows 7*. The program not only protects your computer from viruses, it also offers protection from spyware. |
| **Phishing** | A trap to induce computer users to disclose personal or financial information. A commonly used phishing scam starts with an email message that appears to be sent by a trusted source. The recipients are induced to fill in confidential information on a fake website which may look like an exact copy of a legitimate website. |
| **Quick scan** | An option in an antivirus or antispyware program. When this type of scan is performed, only the locations where unwanted software is most often found will be scanned. |

*- Continue on the next page -*

| | |
|---|---|
| **Real-time-protection** | This function makes sure that *Windows Defender* or *Microsoft Security Essentials* constantly monitors all activity while you are surfing the Internet. Any attempt to install malware on your computer will be blocked. |
| **SmartScreen filter** | The SmartScreen filter in *Internet Explorer* helps to protect you from phishing websites. If a website appears on the list of reported phishing websites, you will see a warning. |
| **Spyware** | This is software that can display advertisements, such as pop-ups, collect personal information about you, or change your computer settings without asking permission. |
| **Trojan horse** | A program that contains or installs an unwanted program. The program appears to be innocent, useful, or interesting, but it is actually harmful when executed. |
| **Unwanted software** | Programs that are designed to damage your computer. Also known as malware. |
| **Virus** | A program that tries to distribute itself and spreads from one computer to another, thereby causing damage by deleting or corrupting data, or that annoys users by displaying messages or changing the information that is displayed on the screen. |
| **Windows Defender** | A complete solution for your Internet security in *Windows 8.1*. The program protects your computer from viruses, but also offers a firewall and protection against spyware. |
| **Windows Update** | A system that checks if you are using the most recent version of *Windows 7* or *8.1*. |
| **Worm** | A program that keeps copying itself, just like a virus. A malicious person can use a worm to take over your computer, for instance. |

*Source: Windows Help and Support*

## Protecting against spyware

You could say that spyware is software that keeps an eye on you. They are usually small programs that are secretly added to your computer when you are installing certain legitimate software programs. In order to induce you to install the software, it is often offered for free on the Internet.

Some manufacturers have the decency to indicate (in very fine print) that certain software will be installed along with their free program, software that will send information to the manufacturers. This is disguised as a service for you as a customer. But spyware is mostly installed in secret, and you will often not even notice it is installed, until an antispyware program alerts you. But you can also pick up spyware on your computer by visiting untrustworthy websites.

There are different kinds of spyware, such as adware, that displays unwanted advertisements on your screen, and keyloggers, that register your keystrokes and pass them on to others through the Internet.

Many antivirus programs search for viruses as well as for spyware. Even so, it is a good idea to use a special antispyware program sometimes. This is because antivirus software is mainly directed at viruses. If you notice that you often see unwanted advertisements on your screen, then the time has come to check your computer with an antispyware program. You can find a summary of current programs on http://anti-spyware-review.toptenreviews.com

It is even better if you prevent these spyware programs from being installed on your computer. You should try to keep an eye on the following things:

- Only acquire software from well-known, trustworthy sites where the programs have been checked for viruses.
- Read the license agreement that goes with the program: sometimes you can find out if any information will be passed on after the software has been installed. This is 'official' spyware.
- Do not install programs that are unexpectedly given to you by others.
- Do not click the buttons in suspicious-looking pop-up windows that appear while you are surfing. It is better to close your browser and/or restart your computer.
- Before you install a program, check whether it contains spyware, by using an antispyware program.

## Secure your hardware

There is more to securing a computer or laptop than just installing an antivirus program or a firewall. Thieves love to steal laptops: expensive and easy to carry along. So you have good reason to protect your computer or notebook in a physical sense as well.

There are various types of cables, locks, and clamps that can protect your device against theft. The cheapest solution is to use a cable. That is to say, a special steel cable with a plastic coating. One end of the cable is equipped with a lock that can be inserted into a special slot in the computer. The other end of the cable is connected to a fixed object that cannot be removed.

Another method of securing your computer is to secure it to a desk with a lock system. A special supporting base is anchored to a desk with very powerful glue. The computer is locked to the base. It will be virtually immovable. Unfortunately this leaves you with a permanent computer lock on your desk, even if you no longer need it for your computer.

If you often travel with your notebook you can buy special notebook cases that protect your device from damage and theft. These cases are made from aluminum, or a combination of aluminum and steel, and equipped with locks that are opened with a key or a number code. These cases may have a cable with which you can anchor it to a fixed object, so it cannot be taken easily.
Apart from that, you can equip your computer with a wireless alarm system, placed on the laptop or the laptop case. After you have set the alarm and the computer or the case is picked up, the alarm will make a loud noise.

It is a good idea to engrave your computer with your name. This makes it easier for the police to recover your belongings, and harder for thieves to sell the device. You can also mark your computer with a tag that is glued to your computer with very strong glue. This tag will contain a unique number code and barcode, by which your computer can always be identified as being your own, in case of loss or theft. If someone tries to take off the tag, the computer will still display a print with the message that it has been stolen, including the number code and a phone number you can call to report the theft.

*- Continue on the next page -*

A method for following your computer live, after it has been stolen, is a tracking system: also called track-and-trace. When a stolen computer connects to the Internet, sooner or later, the software will automatically send a message to the software manufacturer. In turn, the manufacturer will alert a team of specialists, and the local police department, in order to recover your computer.

Yet another option is the GPS Mini Tracker. This is a device you hide in your computer. In case of theft, you can call the number of the tracker with your cell phone. On the screen of your cell phone (or of a connected computer) you will see a map on which the location of the Mini Tracker, that is to say, of your computer, is marked.

These track and trace systems are unfortunately one of the more expensive means of securing your computer.

### Safe mail behavior

There is a lot you can do yourself to prevent infections coming from an email message. A regular email message that contains only words does not pose a big threat. But an attachment included in an email may prove to be dangerous. Fortunately, various types of potentially harmful attachments are blocked by the security settings of your email program. But it still is important that you take a close look at your messages before you open them. Pay attention to the following things:

- Always make sure to use an up-to-date antivirus program.
- Never open messages from unknown senders. Delete them at once.
- The email does not contain text, or text in a foreign language or in bad English, or the text looks strange for any other reason.
- The email contains an attachment and you are asked to open this attachment.
- The email contains a link and you are asked to click it.
- Does the subject of a message seem familiar? Viruses sometimes use old messages and send these to randomly selected addresses of the contacts in an address book. If you think it is an older message, or a message that is not directed at you, then delete it at once. Of course, you can always call the sender.
- Does the message contain an attachment with a strange name, or a strange file type? Do not be curious, delete it at once.
- The attachment is a program file, which you can tell by the extension .EXE, .COM, .PIF or .VBS. If you are in doubt about an attachment, then right-click the file. Next, you click *Save As*. Afterwards you can select the desired folder on your computer and let your antivirus program scan this folder. Make sure not to open the file before you have scanned it.

Remember that deleted messages are stored in the *Junk* folder and that you will need to empty this folder as well.

# 1.12 Tips

 **Tip**

**Delete an update**

Occasionally, an update may cause problems in certain computer configurations. If you cannot solve the problem by restoring the system to a restore point (see *Chapter 3 Creating Backups*), you can remove the update. Only do this if it is recommended by *Microsoft*, or by the manufacturer of the software/hardware that has experienced problems.

☞ **Open the *Control Panel***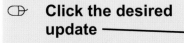

☞ **Click** System and Security

☞ **By** Windows Update, **click**

View update history

**or**

View installed updates

In *Windows 8.1*:

☞ **Click**

Installed Updates.

In both versions:

☞ **Click the desired update** ─────

Look at the number following the update name, and take good care to delete the correct update.

☞ **Click** Uninstall ─────

☞ **If necessary, follow the instructions in the next few windows**

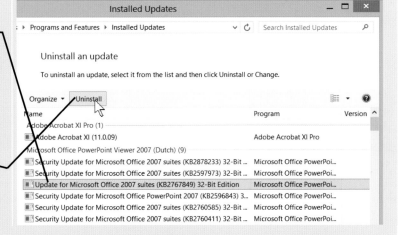

In many cases, the computer will need to be restarted after you have deleted an update.

**Tip**

**Scan a specific folder in your antivirus program**
In this chapter you have done a quick scan with *Windows Defender* or *Microsoft Security Essentials*. A quick scan means the program decides for itself which folders are going to be scanned. If you want to scan a specific folder or drive, such as a USB stick or an external hard drive, you can do that as follows:

☞ **Click the radio button**
  **⦿ by** Custom

☞ **Click** Scan now

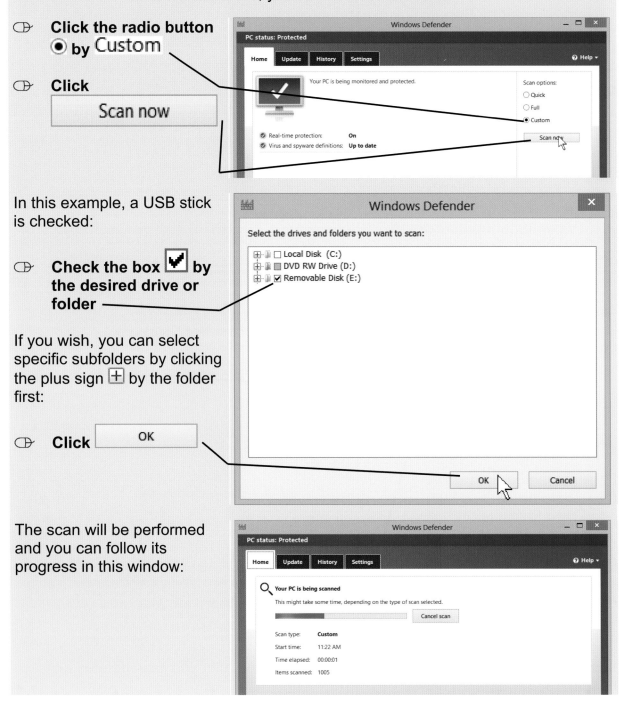

In this example, a USB stick is checked:

☞ **Check the box** ✔ **by the desired drive or folder**

If you wish, you can select specific subfolders by clicking the plus sign ⊞ by the folder first:

☞ **Click** OK

The scan will be performed and you can follow its progress in this window:

# 2. Safeguarding Your Privacy

In the first chapter you have learned about protecting your computer against malicious external influences. In this chapter we explain how to use the Internet in a safe manner. Nowadays, the Internet is not only used for sending email and searching for information, but it has become the main medium for shopping, conducting financial transactions, and contacting others through social network sites.

During all these activities you leave all sorts of traces on the Internet, deliberately but also unknowingly, which can endanger your privacy. In this chapter you will find lots of useful information and tips that will help you protect your privacy while using the Internet.

In this chapter you will learn how to:

- recognize what spam is, and how to prevent it;
- deal with cookies;
- change the privacy settings in Internet browsers;
- delete your browser history;
- create strong passwords and remember them;
- safely conduct your Internet banking business;
- safely shop and pay online;
- safely use *Facebook, Twitter*, and other social media.

# 2.1 What is Spam?

By 'spam' we mean all those email messages containing unwanted and undesirable ads that seem to land in your inbox on a daily basis. These might be ads for ordering certain medication, online gambling, or shady dating websites.

Here you see a few examples of spam:

| From | Subject |
|---|---|
| Viagra Professional Store | The Highest Grade Meds And EXTRA LOW Price ! |
| Be mail | Audi A4 quattro edition. Italia. Land of quattro®. |
| BM per Zurich Connect | RCA: Con Zurich Connect risparmi anche il 40% |
| alize5591148.77154@emailbasura.org | Do you desire to gratify your babe tonight? |
| Be mail | Approfitta in esclusiva della vendita evento DESIGUAL |
| Drugs-Store | SUMMER SALE SEASON STARTED! GRAB EXTRA 11% OFF! |

There are different ways in which your email address can end up on the mailing list for this unwanted email. You may have signed up for an online service, using your email address. The administrators of the service could have added your email address along with lots of others to companies that send spam. These companies also use software that tries to guess the account name of frequently used email addresses (initial.lastname@...) and use robots to search the Internet for email addresses placed on websites.

# 2.2 How Do You Prevent Spam?

If you frequently use the Internet, you cannot avoid having to share your email address every now and then. Entering a contest is only possible if you fill in your name, address and email address, for example. If you need to pass on your annual energy readings electronically to an electricity company, you usually need to create an account with an email address. The same goes for online shopping. It is hard to prevent spam altogether. Yet there are some ways in which you can limit the amount of spam you receive:

- Only give your main email address (the address you use the most, or the one you use in your email program) to the people you trust. Use one or multiple easily replaceable (free) email addresses as a 'disposable address', in case you want to enter contests or create accounts on company websites. You can easily create a new account on *Outlook.com* (formerly called *Hotmail*) or *Gmail*. A free email address can be used to receive the newsletters from businesses, celebrities or online stores. If this address attracts too much spam after a while, you can create a new address.

- Make sure your email address cannot be found on the Internet! Never mention your email address on websites, internet forums, newsgroups, or in communities. Spammers use robots that automatically search the Internet for email addresses.

- Never respond to spam email. Do not reply back, or click the 'unsubscribe' link in the email message.

When you click an 'unsubscribe' link, the senders will know that your email address is correct, and you may receive even more spam:

The same goes for other links in a spam email:

These may lead to phishing websites, or (like in this example) to websites where they try to induce you to play games and gamble at expensive online casinos.

 **Tip**

**Unsubscribe to newsletters**

If you want to unsubscribe to the newsletter you receive from a business you know, you can certainly use the *unsubscribe* or *sign off* link. But make sure to check that the newsletter is actually sent by the company. Many businesses publish their newsletter archives on their website. Here you can easily check whether the newsletter is really theirs, or whether it has been sent by spammers.

- Do you need to send an email to multiple recipients? Then you should hide the addresses of all the recipients. You can do this by entering all the email addresses in the BCC field. In this way, the persons that receive your email will not be able to see who the other recipients are. BCC stands for *Blind Carbon Copy*. This means that you are sending a copy of your message to many people but they cannot see the other persons that are receiving this message.

- Do not forward funny or well-meaning chain letters. When such letters are forwarded, nobody thinks to delete the email addresses of previous recipients. In the end, a chain letter can contain hundreds of email addresses, due to the continuous forwarding of the letter. In the *Tips* at the end of this chapter you can read more about chain letters.

- Use a spam filter. A spam filter will help stop spam email from landing in your *Inbox*. All suspicious email will automatically be moved to the *Junk Mail* folder. In most cases, you will not need to take action yourself, since a spam filter is usually configured by your email service provider. But you will sometimes need to mark a message that has not been recognized by the spam filter as 'spam'. The spam filter will 'learn' along the way, and will block similar messages, next time around.

In the examples below we will be using *Windows Live Mail*. This is a useful, free, and easy-to-use program with extensive options for managing your email. If you use a different email program, you will have similar options for marking an email as spam.

☞ **Open *Windows Live Mail*** 🐾⁸

In this example, one new message has been moved to the *Junk Mail* folder:

☞ **Click** Junk email (1)

It is always possible that a message is unrightfully tagged as spam. It is important to check the content of your *Junk Mail* folder regularly. If a message has been mistakenly moved to the *Junk Mail* folder, you can move it back to the *Inbox*, like this:

☞ **Right-click the message that is not a junk email**

☞ **Click** Junk email

☞ **Click** Mark as not junk

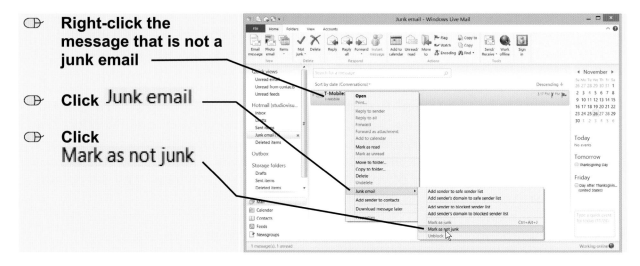

Now the message will be moved to your *Inbox*.

Future messages from this sender may still end up in the *Junk Mail* folder. If you want to prevent this from happening, you can add the sender to the safe senders list:

 **If necessary, click**
Inbox ——————

 **Right-click the message** ——

 **Click** Junk email

 **Click**
Add sender to safe sender list

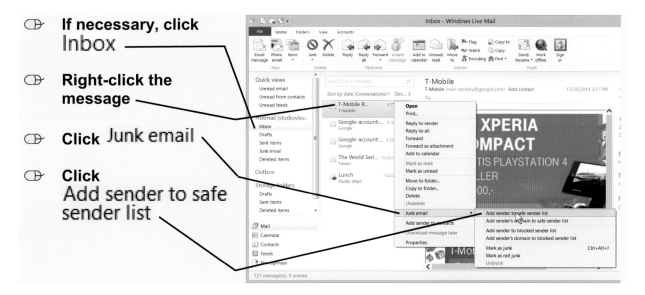

## Tip

**Add a domain**

You can also select the Add sender's domain to safe sender list option. The domain name of the sender is the last part of the email address, for example @nytimes.com, or @visualsteps.com. With this option you can make sure that all the messages sent by this domain are delivered to your *Inbox*.

You should be a bit cautious about using this option, for example, with messages that end in @outlook.com, @hotmail.com and @gmail.com. It is possible for spam to be sent from these well-known domains.

You will see a confirmation:

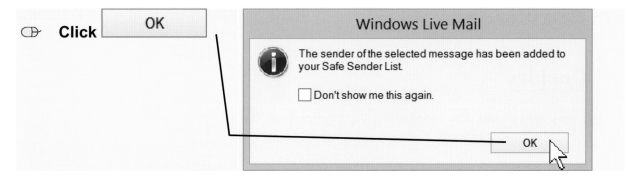 **Click** OK

From now on, the messages from this sender will be delivered to your *Inbox*.

It is still possible that a spam email is not recognized and ends up in your regular *Inbox*. This is how you can mark the email as junk:

☞ **Right-click the message**

☞ **Click** Junk email, Mark as junk

*Windows Live Mail* will ask if the junk email has to be reported. By enabling this option, it can help the spam filter to recognize more junk email.

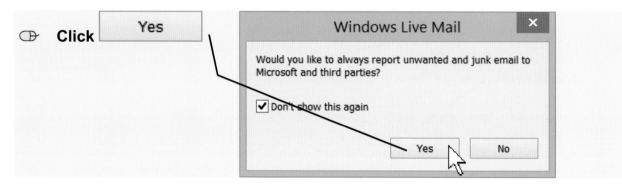

The message is moved to the *Junk Mail* folder.

If you want to move all the messages from this sender to the *Junk Mail* folder from now on, you can add the sender to the blocked sender list:

☞ **Right-click the message**

☞ **Click** Junk email

☞ **Click** Add sender to blocked sender list

☞ **Close** *Windows Live Mail* ✂️¹

## 2.3 Cookies

When you visit a website, cookies will be stored on your computer. The main object of a cookie is to distinguish between different users.

Cookies do not pose a threat to the operation of your computer. They do not damage files or programs. Nor can they access your files. In fact, they are just simple text files and not programs.

The main types of cookies are:

- functional cookies: these are necessary in order to get the website to function properly. For instance, a cookie that remembers your login name, or makes sure you stay logged in, or saves the content of your shopping cart in a webshop. These are also called *first party cookies*. These are cookies that are generated by the website itself.

- analytic cookies: these cookies register how often a website is visited, or how often an ad is clicked. These cookies can be generated by the website owner, or by third parties. These are also called *third party cookies*.

- tracking cookies: these are cookies that make it possible to track the websites people visit on the Internet. These cookies are put in place by an advertiser who has obtained permission from the website owner, for example. If this advertiser can put his cookies on multiple websites, he can deduce which websites have been visited by the same user. This is useful information which can be used to point ads to specific users. These are third party cookies as well. For example, tracking cookies make sure that when you have searched information on a television set on website A, website B suddenly display ads by companies that sell television sets.

Since May 2012, the so-called Cookie Law has come into action in the EU countries. This law requires websites to inform its visitors about the kinds of cookies that are in use on their websites, and for what purpose. The websites need to obtain informed consent of each visitor, before being allowed to place the cookies. The law does not apply to companies that operate exclusively within the US, but if they target European users they will have to comply too. Recently, there has been a lot of discussion and complaints about this law from the local business community.

Asking for the visitor's permission is done in various ways. For example, a bar may be displayed above or below the window, as is seen in this example from the http://www.bbc.com/ website.

No permission is required for functional cookies, such as a shopping cart or a login form:

In this case you give permission for different types of cookies, by just continuing to browse. —

If you click click here, you will see additional information on the types of cookies used by this site.

☞  **Click** click here

☞  **Drag the scroll box downwards** —

At the bottom of the page, you can click http://tools.google.com/dlpage to opt out from being tracked by *Google Analytics* tracking cookies:

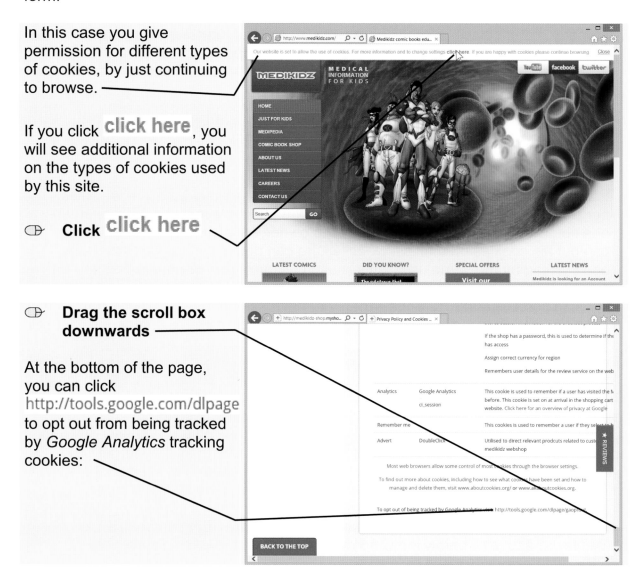

*Google* is known for collecting a lot of data. The company claims to collect this data in order to provide better service to their users. In reality, this mainly means that *Google* is entitled to store all your data. This information is used for creating user profiles, which in turn are used for selling ads. The *Google* search engine will also filter the search results on the basis of items that may be interesting to you. If you are looking for a garage to service your car, and the search results contain a number of garages in your own neighborhood, this might even be useful.

# 2.4 Privacy Settings

In *Internet Explorer* you can let the browser block any cookies, if you wish. This also goes for the cookies on websites where you have previously given permission to use cookies. You should take into account that this may limit the functionality of a website. This is how you block cookies in *Internet Explorer*:

☞ **Open *Internet Explorer*** ⚭⁴

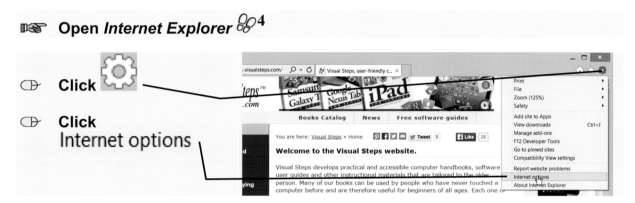

⊕ **Click** ⚙

⊕ **Click**
   Internet options

You will see the *Internet options* window:

⊕ **Click the**
   Privacy **tab**

The default setting is
**Medium**:

⊕ **Drag the slider
   upwards**

The **Medium High** setting
will block third party cookies,
but your shopping cart and
login name will still be
remembered, for example.

**Please note:** the phrase
'...*contact you without your
implicit consent*' in this
respect means that a website
is able to read the cookies
that are stored on your
computer. It does not mean
you will receive phone calls.

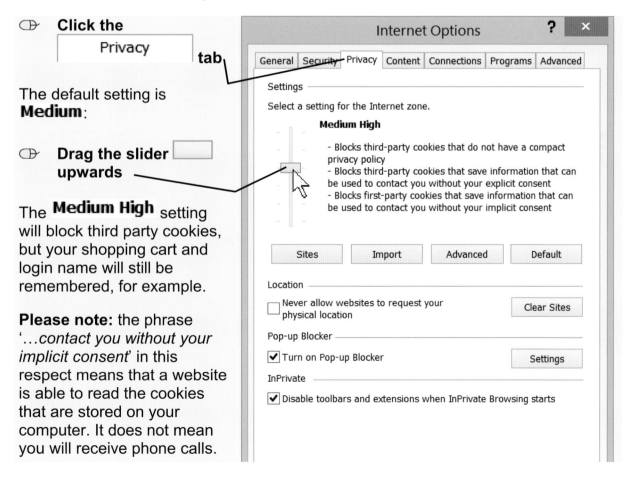

There are five levels: *Accept all cookies*, *Low*, *Medium*, *Medium High*, *High*, and *Block all cookies*. By the slider you can read a description for each level.

You can go back to the default setting:

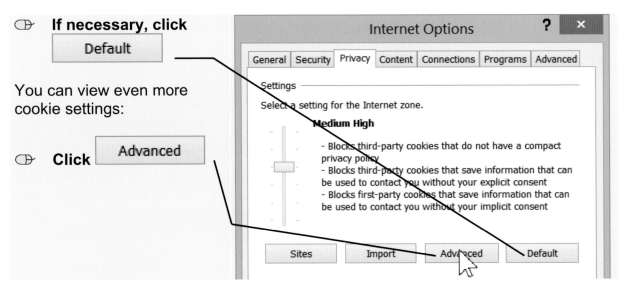

☞ **If necessary, click**
   Default

You can view even more cookie settings:

☞ **Click** Advanced

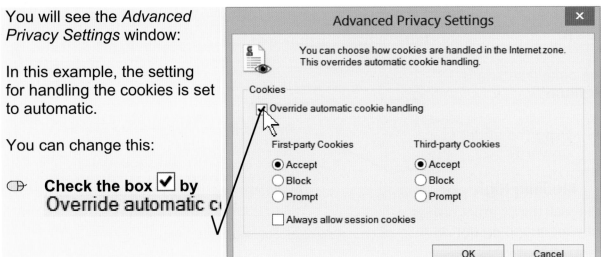

You will see the *Advanced Privacy Settings* window:

In this example, the setting for handling the cookies is set to automatic.

You can change this:

☞ **Check the box ☑ by**
   **Override automatic c**

Now you can take a better look at the options. You can determine exactly what to do with *first party cookies* (functional cookies) and *third party cookies* (analytic cookies and tracking cookies):

- **Accept**: cookies will be handled automatically.
- **Block**: not a single cookie will be accepted.
- **Prompt**: you will receive a message for each cookie, and you will be asked whether you want to block or accept it, every single time.

*First party cookies* originate from the websites you visit, and they can be permanent or temporary. A temporary cookie will be deleted from *Internet Explorer* when you close the program. A permanent cookie is stored on your computer and will remain stored. This way, the cookie can be read when you view the same website again.

*Third party cookies* are generated by the ads on the websites you visit (such as *pop-ups* and *banners*). Websites can use these cookies to monitor your surfing behavior, and use this information for marketing purposes.

It is better to select the original setting again:

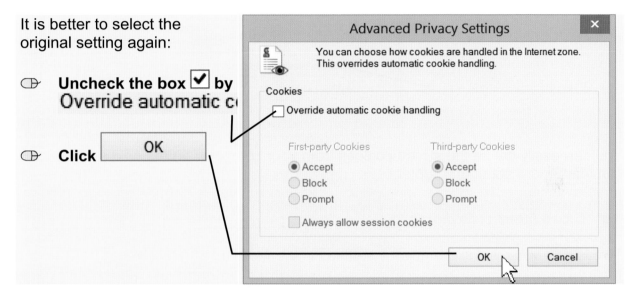

 **Uncheck the box ☑ by Override automatic c**

 **Click** ☐ OK

In the *Internet options* window:

 **Click** ☐ OK

**➥ Please note:**
You may prefer to block all cookies. If you do this, there is a chance of some websites not working properly. But you can always experiment with different settings. If you do not like it, you can select another option.

**💡 Tip**
**Always allow session cookies**
Some websites use cookies while you are visiting the website, but will remove them afterwards. These are called *session cookies*. Session cookies are also called temporary cookies, because they are removed from your computer when you close *Internet Explorer*. Session cookies are used for online banking, for instance. If you have set all cookies to be blocked, including the session cookies, you will no longer be able to log on to these websites. The website will display a warning message.

*- Continue on the next page -*

This is why you should
always check the box ☑ by
Always allow session cookie
Even if you block the other
cookies:

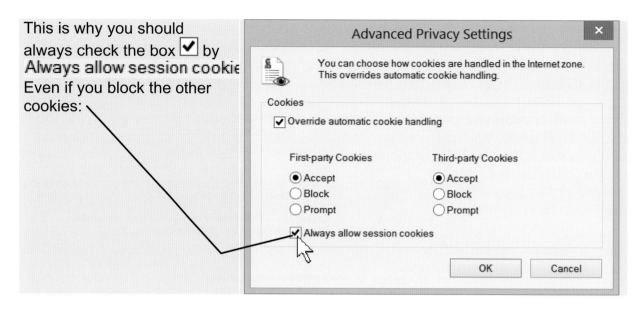

You can easily delete the stored cookies from your computer. In the next section you
can learn more about this subject.

☞ **Close *Internet Explorer*** 🐾¹

This is how you display the privacy settings in the *Mozilla Firefox* browser:

☞ **Open *Mozilla Firefox*, if you wish** 🐾⁵

If the menu bar is not visible:

  ☞ **Right-click a blank
section beside the tab**

  ☞ **Click** Menu Bar

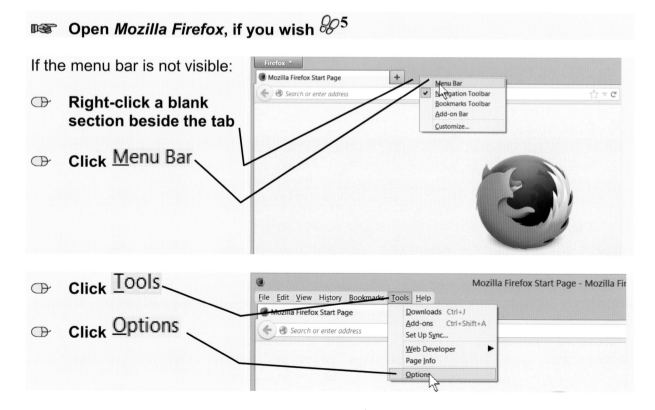

  ☞ **Click** Tools

  ☞ **Click** Options

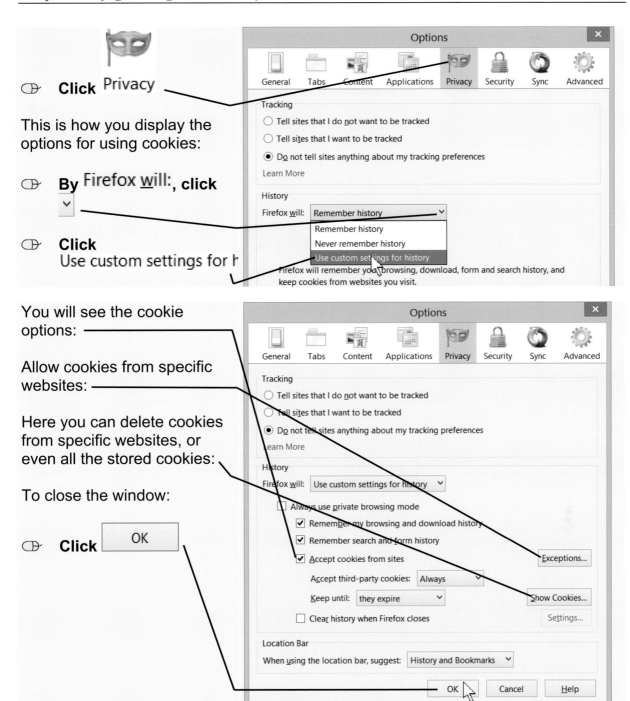

⊕  **Click** Privacy

This is how you display the options for using cookies:

⊕  **By** Firefox will:**, click** ˅

⊕  **Click**
Use custom settings for h

You will see the cookie options: ——————

Allow cookies from specific websites: ——————

Here you can delete cookies from specific websites, or even all the stored cookies:

To close the window:

⊕  **Click** OK

☞  **Close** *Mozilla Firefox* 🦶¹

This is how you display the privacy options in *Google Chrome*:

☞  **Open** *Google Chrome*, **if you wish** 🦶⁶

Click ☰

Click Settings

Drag the scroll box downwards

Click
Show advanced settings

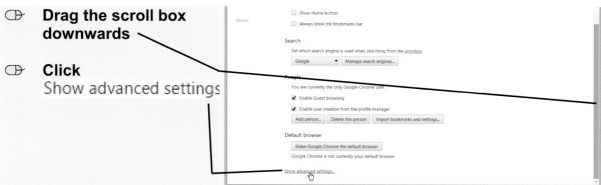

Drag the scroll box downwards

By Privacy you will see the privacy and security options:

Click
Content settings...

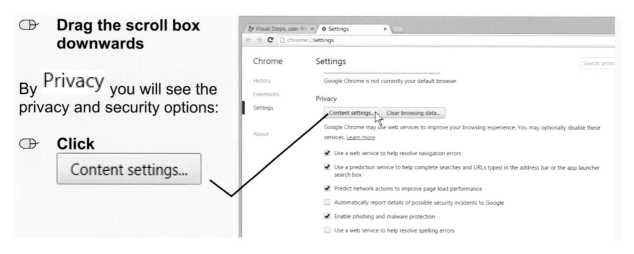

You will see the options for allowing cookies:

Click [Manage exceptions...] if you want to: allow cookies from specific websites, delete them upon exiting the website, or block them:

If you want to delete cookies, use the [All cookies and site data...] option:

After you have changed the settings:

☞  **Click** [Done]

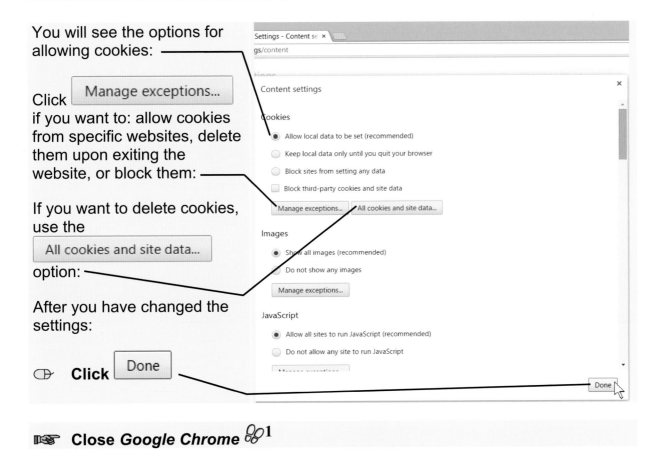

☞  **Close** *Google Chrome* 👣[1]

# 2.5 Deleting the Browser History

When you browse the Internet, *Internet Explorer* stores information regarding the websites you visit. You can also save the data you enter on a website, such as your name and address, for example. The browser history consists of various items. The main items are:

- **Temporary Internet files and website files**: the first time you visit a web page, it is stored in the folder with *Temporary Internet Files*. This means the pages can be displayed much quicker if you visit them again, since *Internet Explorer* will now be able to open them from the cached files in the folder. Only the changed content needs to be downloaded.
- **Cookies and website data**: small text files generated by the websites you have visited. They are stored on your computer in order to save information about you and your preferences.
- **History**: a list of all the websites you have visited.

- **Form data** : information you have entered in forms on websites, or in the address bar, such as your name, address, and web addresses.
- **Passwords** : every time you enter a password on a website, *Internet Explorer* will ask you if it needs to be saved. These saved passwords can be deleted as well.

Usually it is quite handy to have all this information stored on your computer. It may enhance your surfing speed, or provide information automatically, so you will not need to type certain data over and over again. But you may want to get rid of this information when you decide to clean up your computer. If you are using a public computer and do not want to leave personal information behind on that computer, you can delete this data.

This is how you delete the browser history:

☞ **Open** *Internet Explorer* 🐾4

⊕  **Click** ⚙

⊕  **Click** Safety

⊕  **Click**
    Delete browsing history

In the next window you can select which part of the browser history to delete. Each item has a description that explains its content.

The items that are checked
✔, will be deleted:

⊕ **Check the boxes** ✔ **by**
**the desired items**

⊕ **Click** Delete

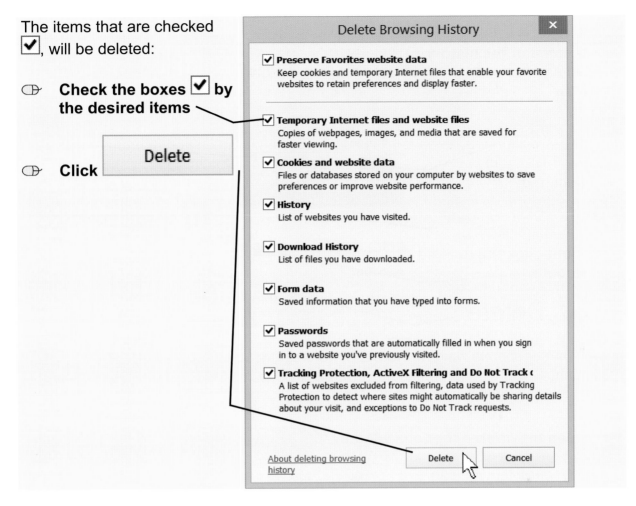

**Delete Browsing History** ✕

☑ **Preserve Favorites website data**
Keep cookies and temporary Internet files that enable your favorite
websites to retain preferences and display faster.

☑ **Temporary Internet files and website files**
Copies of webpages, images, and media that are saved for
faster viewing.

☑ **Cookies and website data**
Files or databases stored on your computer by websites to save
preferences or improve website performance.

☑ **History**
List of websites you have visited.

☑ **Download History**
List of files you have downloaded.

☑ **Form data**
Saved information that you have typed into forms.

☑ **Passwords**
Saved passwords that are automatically filled in when you sign
in to a website you've previously visited.

☑ **Tracking Protection, ActiveX Filtering and Do Not Track** 
A list of websites excluded from filtering, data used by Tracking
Protection to detect where sites might automatically be sharing details
about your visit, and exceptions to Do Not Track requests.

About deleting browsing
history

Delete    Cancel

## ➦ **Please note:**

If you use the *Internet Explorer* app in *Windows 8.1*, the browser history of this app
will be deleted as well.

You will see a small confirmation window. You can close this window:

⊕ **Click** ✕

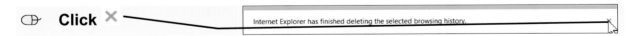

Internet Explorer has finished deleting the selected browsing history.

## 💡 Tip

### Delete some of the history

You can also remove individual websites from the browser history. You can do that like this:

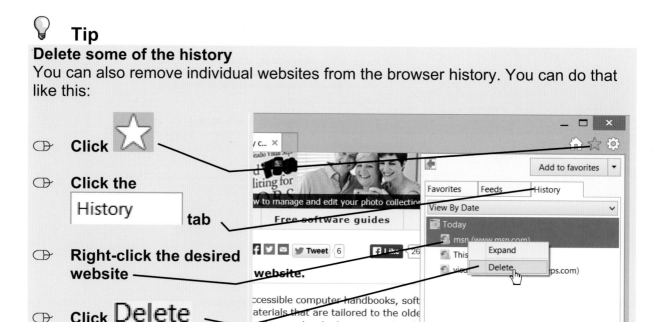

☞ **Click** ⭐

☞ **Click the** `History` **tab**

☞ **Right-click the desired website**

☞ **Click** Delete

In the *Internet options* window there are more settings that you can adjust.
For instance, you can determine for how many days the websites you have visited will be saved in the browser history:

👉 **Open the *Internet options* window** 👣[9]

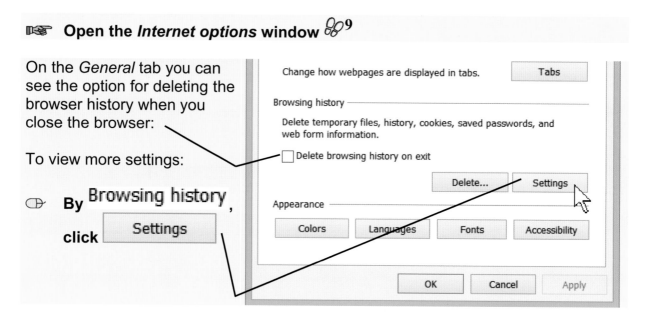

On the *General* tab you can see the option for deleting the browser history when you close the browser:

To view more settings:

☞ **By** `Browsing history`, **click** Settings

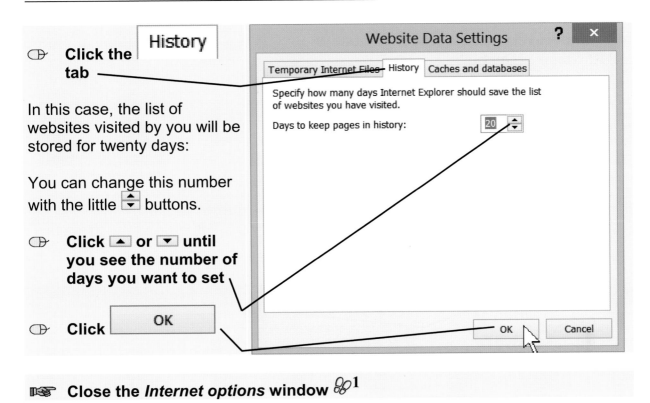

☞ **Click the** **History** **tab**

In this case, the list of websites visited by you will be stored for twenty days:

You can change this number with the little ⬍ buttons.

☞ **Click ▲ or ▼ until you see the number of days you want to set**

☞ **Click** OK

☞ **Close the *Internet options* window** 👣**1**

After you have deleted the history, the folder will be empty. You can check this for yourself:

☞ **Click** ☆

☞ **Click the** **History** **tab**

You can see that the list is blank:

All the web addresses (URLs) of the websites you have recently visited, have been deleted from memory.

☞ **Close *Internet Explorer*** 👣**1**

This is how you delete the browser history in the *Mozilla Firefox* browser:

☞ **Open *Mozilla Firefox*, if you wish** 👣**5**

 **If necessary, display the menu bar** &⚏7

Click **History**

Display the history: —————

Delete the history: —————

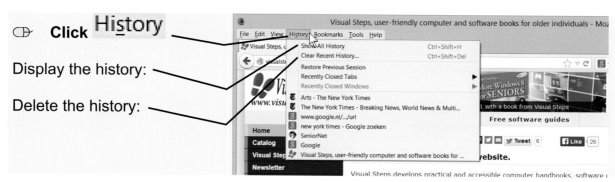

This is how you find the options for setting up the browser history:

Click **Tools**

Click **Options**

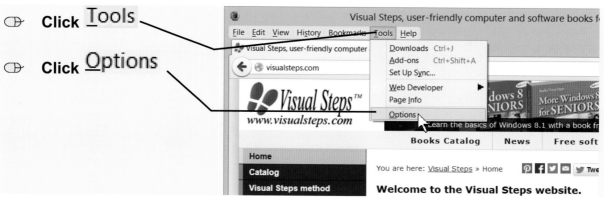

Click **Privacy**

By default, *Mozilla Firefox* will remember the browser history. To change this:

By **Firefox will:** , click ⌄

Click Use custom settings for hi

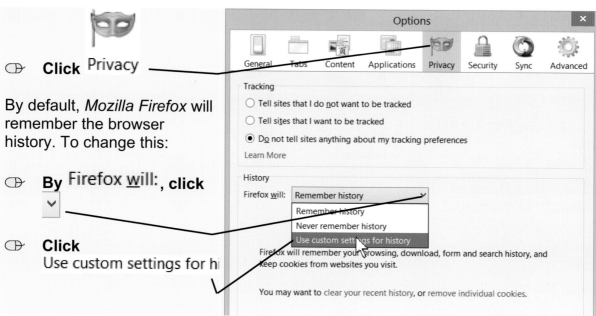

By default, the navigation and download history is remembered: —————

The search and form history is saved as well: —————

You will also see an option for deleting the history when you close *Mozilla Firefox*:

To close the window:

☞ **Click** OK

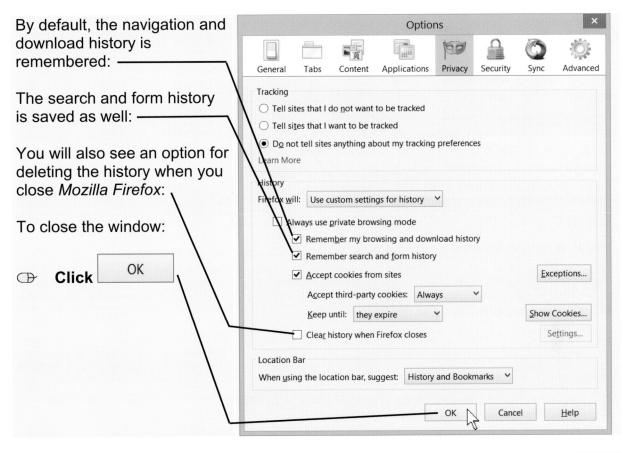

☞ **Close *Mozilla Firefox*** 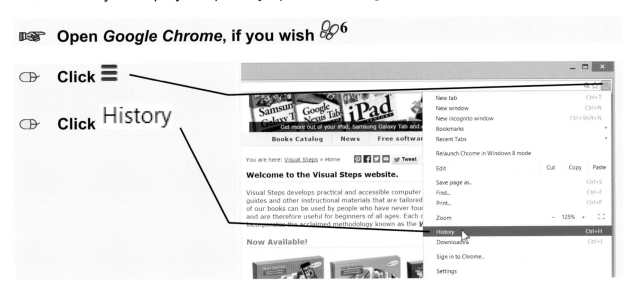¹

This is how you display the privacy options in *Google Chrome*:

☞ **Open *Google Chrome*, if you wish** ⸜⸝⁶

☞ **Click** ≡

☞ **Click** History

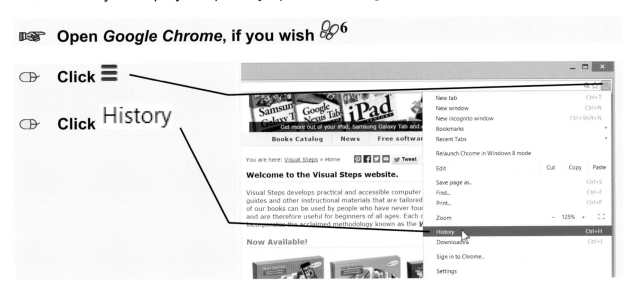

The previously opened websites are displayed:

You can delete the full browser history with

If you just want to delete some specific websites, you select these websites and then click

Remove selected items :

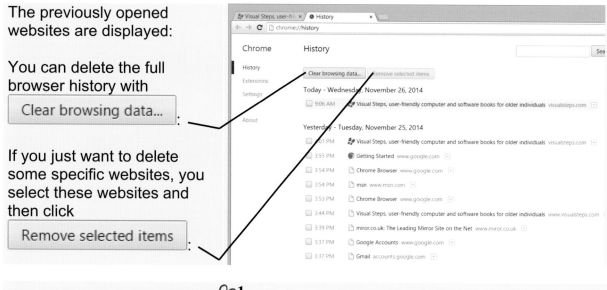

☞ Close *Google Chrome* ✂¹

 **Tip**

**CCleaner**
With the free *CCleaner* program you can clean up the temporary Internet files on your computer quickly and safely. You can also remove other types of redundant data that can clutter your hard drive. This program cleans the drive more thoroughly than the built-in clean-up tools in *Windows*. In *Chapter 4 Cleaning Up Your Computer* you can read more about this useful program.

## 2.6 Choosing Strong Passwords

Most Internet services require you to create an account, such as the account you create in a webshop, if you want to buy something. An account consists of a user name, password and possibly other information. You will need your username and password to sign in to the webshop or Internet service. The user name is often your email address. The password is something you need to make up yourself.

It is recommended not to use your main email address for all these different accounts. There is always a possibility that the email addresses used for creating an account are collected and passed on to third parties. This can result in a sharp increase in the amount of spam received by the email address. It is better to use one or more easily replaceable email addresses as a 'disposable' address, in order to create such accounts. It is easy to create free email addresses on *Outlook.com* (formerly known as *Hotmail*) or *Gmail*.

A password is a combination of numbers and letters, and sometimes other punctuation marks, with which your data is secured on the Internet. It is the 'key' to access your data. Passwords are used to access your email, your account with the energy company, your Internet subscription, but also for your banking activities on the Internet. A password makes sure that you are the only one who can access your personal data.

It is extremely important to choose a 'secure' password. If somebody else were to guess your password, a hacker, for example, he can access and change all your data. You have to try to prevent this. Most websites allow you to choose your own password. Sometime a password is issued by the website. It is a good idea to change this password immediately, once you have logged in for the first time.

It is tempting to choose a password that is easy to remember, and use the same password for multiple services. But this puts you at risk. Cybercriminals steal passwords on websites with poor security and then try to use the same passwords and usernames on other, more secure websites, such as a banker's website.

If you pay close attention to the creation of your password and keep using different passwords, your data will be better protected.

These are obvious passwords that can be guessed quickly by the computer programs used by hackers:

- number sequences: 123456, 0123456789
- letter sequences: abcdef
- number and letter sequences: abc123
- repeated characters: 88888888, pppppp
- letters that are next to each other on your keyboard: qwerty, fghjkl
- obvious words: secret, password, welcome
- a combination of your first name and year of birth: Anne1950
- personal data: your passport number, date of birth, license plate number
- (difficult) words taken out of a dictionary, no matter what language
- words spelled the other way round
- incorrectly spelled words

Many Internet services do not impose very strict requirements for the passwords you use, which allows you to use an obvious password such as Anne1950:

Create password

8-character minimum; case sensitive

Reenter password

Passwords must have at least 8 characters and contain at least two of the following: uppercase letters, lowercase letters, numbers, and symbols.

Do not use the same password for different accounts. The security of the data you enter with various Internet services (large or small) is not 100% guaranteed. If the secure password you have used for one of these services is hacked, you will need to change your password on all the other websites as well, in order to prevent people from abusing your accounts.

A good way of creating secure passwords for different services is to use a *basic password* to which you add another word for each service you use. The basic password needs to be easy to remember for you, but difficult to guess for others. That is why it is recommended to use at least eight characters, and construct the basic password from a combination of letters, punctuation marks, symbols, and numbers.

There are different methods for making a basic password. Two examples:

- Think of a word, for example, 'garbagebin'. You replace some of the characters in this word and turn it into 'G3rba8eB@n'. If you want to use this trick, then make sure that the basic password cannot be easily guessed by others, so do not use your place of birth, or your favorite car brand.

- If you want to make your basic password even more difficult, then think of a sentence that you can easily remember. This can be a proverb, or a song line. Use the first letter of each word in that sentence to construct your password. For instance, use the sentence 'this is a letter to my mother in heaven'. The password would be: 'tialtmmih'. Then you put your lucky number in front of the password, replace the letter 'i' by a '%' symbol, and replace two other letters by capital letters. Now the password has become this: 5t%aLtMM%h

For each service you use, you should add a unique word or character to your basic password. You can make this as complicated as you wish. For example:

- Your basic password is 'G3rba8eB@n'. For the Amazon webshop you can add the word 'hippo' to this password. The new password will become: 'G3rba8eB@nhippo'. Use another word for the Shoes.com webshop, for instance, 'fruit bowl'. The password will then become 'G3rba8eB@nfruitbowl'

- If you have based your basic password on the initial letters of the words in a sentence, you can take this method a bit further. Try to think of a short sentence for each individual service, and then use the first letter of this short sentence and add it to the basic password. For example, the sentences 'Gmail is useful' for your Gmail account, or 'Amazon has a lot of books' for your Amazon account. With Gmail, your password will become: 5t%aLtMM%hGiu

There are lots of other tricks you can think of, but no matter what you choose, always make sure it is difficult for others to guess.

 **Tip**

**Secret question**
Websites often have an option for setting up a 'secret question' or 'security question' when you create an account. You can use the answer to a personal question to reset your password later on, in case you have forgotten it.
It is not wise to do this. The answers to these questions are often easy to look up. For example: what is your mother's maiden name? What is your place of birth? If a website forces you to set up a secret question, you could use a version of your basic password as the answer.

# 2.7 Remembering Passwords

If you use the Internet a lot, the number of passwords you need to remember for all the online services will rapidly grow. There are various methods for remembering these passwords:

- write down your passwords;
- let *Internet Explorer* remember your passwords;
- use an online password management service, such as *LastPass*.

The first option for remembering your passwords is to write them down on a piece of paper or in a notebook, and store it somewhere safe. Some security experts think that the risk of your computer being hacked and the resulting loss of private information are greater than the risk of being burgled and losing your notes on the passwords. But it is not very sensible to physically stick a note with all your passwords on your computer.

If you decide to write down your passwords, you need to make sure your document is safely hidden, and others should not be able to understand what the document is about. Also, you should never write down the entire password for a specific website. Try to make it as incomprehensible as possible for others. Like this, for example:

- do not write down your basic password, but remember it;
- only write down the extra words you have added to your basic password, for all the different services. So: 'Amazon – hippo' or 'Shoes – fruit bowl';
- if you are using the sentence-method, you can just write down 'Gmail is useful', or 'Amazon has a lot of books'.

Since you have only written down the additional words for each account, and not the basic password, this method of choosing and remembering your passwords is still a secure one.

It is not a good idea to let *Internet Explorer* remember your passwords:

These passwords will also be available for others using your computer. *Internet Explorer* does not encrypt these passwords when it saves them, so if a hacker gains access to your computer, the passwords that are stored can be accessed as well.

👆 **Click**
**Not for this site**

Another method for remembering your passwords is using an online management service, such as *LastPass. LastPass* is a free online service that remembers all the passwords for the websites you use, within a single account. Every time you sign in with a new website, the program will ask you whether the data have to be remembered. If you do this, afterwards the data will be entered automatically.

When you install *LastPass* you need to set up a master password:

**Please note:** you cannot retrieve your *LastPass* password, if you forget it! But *LastPass* will send you an email with the reminder you entered when installing the program.

Make sure that this reminder is incomprehensible to others. It should not be easy for a hacker to decipher it.

## Create a LastPass Account

**Email**
name@provider.com

**Master Password**
•••••••••

Password Strength

**Confirm Master Password**
•••••••••

**Master Password Reminder**

☑ I agree to: Terms of Service
Privacy Statement

Back    Create Account

You can also allow LastPass to search for unsecured passwords on your computer.

To import the passwords:

⊕ **Click** Import

These passwords will be added to your *LastPass* vault. Once this has been done, you can decide whether you want to delete these passwords from your computer.

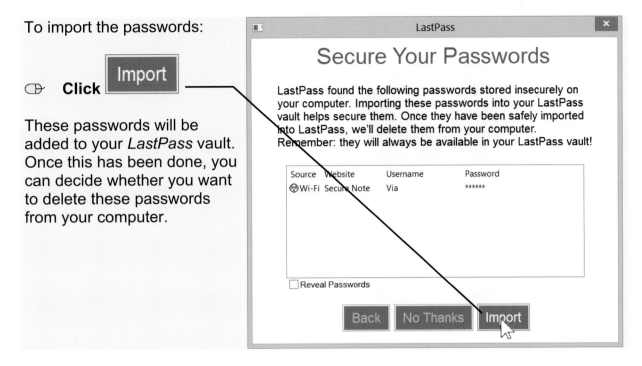

The LastPass browser add-on (toolbar) has been installed onto the internet browser:

You are asked to enable the *LastPass Toolbar*:

⊕ **Click** Enable

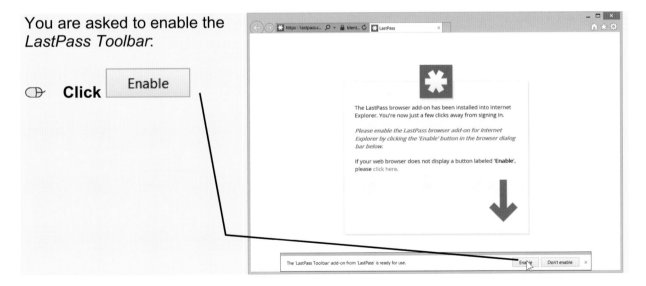

Click

The *LastPass master Login* window appears:

Here you can sign in with your email address and *LastPass* master password. Once you have signed in, the *LastPass* icon will turn into

.

When you sign in with a website, *LastPass* will ask you if the password should be remembered:

Click **Save Site**

If you wish, you can create folders for different groups of passwords:

Click **Save Site**

Now the password has been saved. If you have signed off, signing in again will be very simple:

If you have signed in with your *LastPass* master password, your user name and password will be filled in automatically:

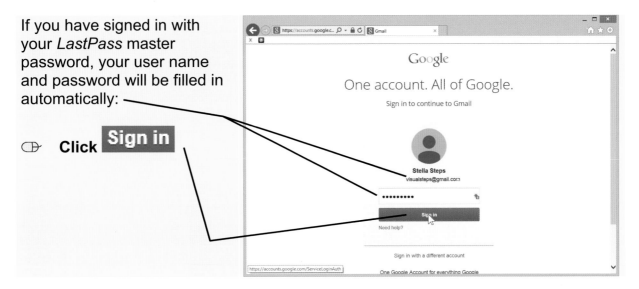

☞  **Click** **Sign in**

*LastPass* can be used with all browser applications, such as *Internet Explorer*, *Mozilla Firefox*, *Google Chrome*, *Safari*, and *Opera*. There are also apps for the iPad, Android tablets and smartphones.

If you install *LastPass* both on your home computer and at work, *LastPass* will synchronize your passwords through the Internet. Because of this, the passwords you save while being at work, will also be available on your home computer.

The passwords are saved and encrypted on your own computer. Only these encrypted passwords are uploaded to *LastPass*. *LastPass* asserts that the key to your passwords is not saved by *LastPass*, which means that the encrypted personal data they store in their database is actually meaningless. All the encryption/decryption procedures are performed on your computer, not through the Internet or on the *LastPass* servers. Nevertheless, these types of services will still be attractive to hackers. Should they ever succeed in accessing your data, then they will have retrieved lots of passwords at once and will know how to use them.

# 2.8 Safe Internet Banking

In *Chapter 1 Protecting Your Computer* you learned about phishing, a method frequently used by criminals in an effort to get hold of your security codes for online banking, for example. Most banks have taken preventive measures to counteract fraudulent activities, but you have some responsibility in this as well. If you do not comply with a number of rules and you become a victim, your bank may decide not to compensate you for the damage.

Adhere to these five basic rules:

1. Keep your security codes hidden.
2. Make sure nobody else ever uses your bank card.
3. Make sure the devices you use for conducting your banking business are safe and well-protected.
4. Check your bank account.
5. Immediately report any incidents to the bank and follow their instructions.

The UK government has launched a campaign to fight against so-called cyber criminals. Other governments around the world are taking similar actions.
The 'Cyber Streetwise' campaign is part of the National Cyber Security Programme.

On the accompanying website, https://www.cyberstreetwise.com, you can find more information about this campaign:

On this interactive website you will see a fictitious street and you can watch videos and get tips on Internet security:

These are the five essential tips for cyber safety:
1.      Install updates.
2.      Install antivirus software.
3.      Use strong passwords.
4.      Shop online safely.
5.      Monitor your social privacy settings.

These are few of the topics discussed on this website:

1. Creating and storing secure passwords and keeping your identity safe.
2. Banking safely on various devices, shopping and paying safely online.
3. Creating a safe wireless network.
4. Safety measures to protect your children's identity.
5. Keeping your computer and devices safe, healthy, and up-to-date.
6. Using social media responsibly.
7. What to do if you are infected.

In the US, there are organizations and alliances set up to inform and educate the public such as the National Cyber Security Alliance with its StaySafeOnline website: http://staysafeonline.org. The FDIC is the closest thing to something on the federal level. The Department of Homeland Security also tries to raise awareness about cyber security with the National Cyber Security Awareness Month. The individual States also have their own policies and laws as well.

You can see that the protection of your computer is a major issue, just as important as keeping your *Windows* operating system and other programs up-to-date. In *Chapter 1 Protecting Your Computer* you can read more about that subject.

Besides the above, it is important to keep a close watch on a number of other things:

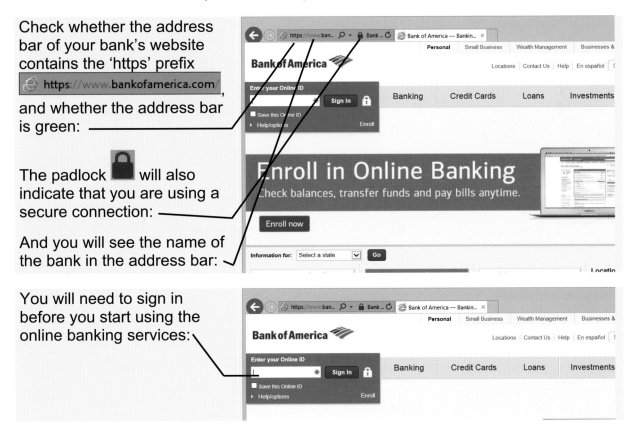

Check whether the address bar of your bank's website contains the 'https' prefix and whether the address bar is green:

The padlock will also indicate that you are using a secure connection:

And you will see the name of the bank in the address bar:

You will need to sign in before you start using the online banking services:

Webshops will also display the green address bar and the padlock. But many websites will have a secure area along with an area that is less safe. For instance, if you are browsing the catalog on www.amazon.com or www.ipgbook.com, the pages are not secure. But, as soon as you want to pay for a book you enter the secured part of the website with https:// in the address bar. There you need to sign in with your username and password. When you actually have reached the stage where

you need to pay for your purchase, you will see the padlock 🔒 too.

A website that displays a padlock 🔒 in the address bar contains a so-called security certificate. These certificates are issued by an independent organization, and guarantee the identity of an external computer such as your bank or a webshop.

☞ **Open *Internet Explorer*** 👣⁴

☞ **If necessary, open the Internet banking section on your bank's website**

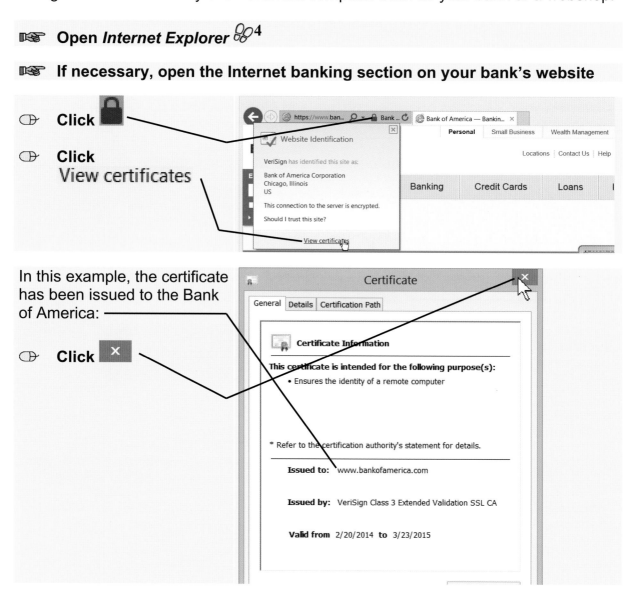

In this example, the certificate has been issued to the Bank of America:

**Please note:**

In the last few sections we have discussed a variety of online safety tips. One thing we cannot stress enough though is how important it is to remain alert when you do any online banking. If strange items appear on the website, and you do not trust things, do not proceed further. Log out and contact your bank.

In the next section you can read more about shopping on the Internet. You will see that the rules that apply to online banking are just as important for online shopping.

# 2.9 Safe Online Shopping

You can buy all sorts of things on the Internet. Books, washing machines, bicycles cars, jewelry, computers, clothes, much more than we can list here. You can book your vacation or day trip, and pay for it on the Internet. You can even use the Internet to search for computer programs and purchase them online. Later you can download and install them. All you need to do is enter your personal information on and the payment will be processed. In a short time, usually less than a day, you will be notified about your order. Then in just a few days it will be delivered to your home. There is no need for you to ever leave your house.

This is all very handy, but take care when you are shopping online. Take the same precautions as you do with online banking when you pay for your purchases.

The first thing to check is the reliability of the webshop you visit. Does the webshop actually deliver the goods you have purchased? A seal of approval, logo (or hallmark) is posted on many webshops to help you recognize this.

There are several seals in use, such as the Better Business Bureau and the Trust-e logo:

Some online shops such as L.L. Bean, for instance, have a sort of sticker that guarantees secure online shopping:

If a webshop has been awarded such a seal of approval, the webshop promises the customers to offer a certain degree of service when things go wrong while ordering or delivering goods.

In the United States, there are a variety of laws at both the federal and state levels that regulate consumer affairs. Among them are the federal Fair Debt Collection Practices Act, the Fair Credit Reporting Act, Truth in Lending Act, Fair Credit Billing Act, and the Gramm-Leach-Bliley Act. Federal consumer protection laws are mainly enforced by the Federal Trade Commission, the Consumer Financial Protection Bureau, and the U.S. Department of Justice.
The majority of states also have a Department of Consumer Affairs devoted to regulating certain industries and protecting consumers who use goods and services from those industries.

Many products and services have been reviewed by Consumer Reports, which gives you an idea of the reliability of online shops. Consumer Reports is not a national institution, you need to become a member to access and benefit from the information. They are a rating service that reviews anything from cars, appliances, electronics, home and garden, to financial services, and more. Their website is at www.ConsumerReports.org.
On a local level there is a popular alternative called Angie's List. This is handy when you need to find a local plumber, painter or other service in your local area.
Angie's List: http://www.angieslist.com/quick-tour.htm.

Many online shops offer information about their guarantee (usually 100% satisfaction guaranteed, or the like), safe online shopping, privacy and security measures and other legal information. You do sometimes have to look for it, though. Usually, there will be a help or support section with a lot of different topics.

On the http://www.bbb.org website you can search for businesses that are BBB accredited. In this way you can check whether the webshop you visit is trustworthy.

If the webshop does not have any seal of approval, you should carefully check out the business. The business name, address and phone number should be listed. You can use *Google Search* or the phone book to look up this information, but even if you do find something it does not guarantee that the business is 100% legitimate.

Another idea is to visit comparison websites, such as www.shopping.com, or www.kelkoo.com, and read about the experiences of other buyers in order to find out if a certain webshop is reliable. These comparison websites also mention which webshops sell the same product too, and at what price. This way, it is easy to find out which webshop offers the best deal. Some webshops also use hallmarks or seals they have invented themselves. That is why it is recommended to thoroughly check out the webshops you want to do business with.

When you choose a webshop, you can also pay attention to the shipping costs they charge. These may vary a lot, from one shop to another. And it is wise to check the options for returning goods and all the other general terms and conditions too, provided they are clearly mentioned on the site. This will save you from unpleasant surprises after ordering a product or other merchandise.

The next issue is the technical security of the webshop, although this is something that will be difficult to check. Is the system in which the webshop has been built, secure and protected from any unauthorized hacks by cybercriminals? If a webshop is awarded one of the legitimate seals of approval, they are usually required to carry out regular security checks and report their security status.

Apart from this, it is important that you keep your computer and browser software up-to-date by installing the most recent updates. Also make sure that your firewall is active and your antivirus program has been updated with the latest definitions. You should also be performing a virus scan at regular intervals.

Furthermore, it is recommended that you only use a Wi-Fi network that is secured with a password. This will prevent others from using your Wi-Fi connection. You should not use a computer you have borrowed or a public computer in an Internet café if you are sending personal or private information over the Internet. You usually have no idea what kind of security measures have been taken.

Many webshops require you to create an account when you want to purchase something for the first time. You can often choose your own password for this account. For this you can use the tips we described in *section 2.6 Choosing Strong Passwords*. Choose a unique, strong password and be sure not to use the same password for other services, such as your email service.

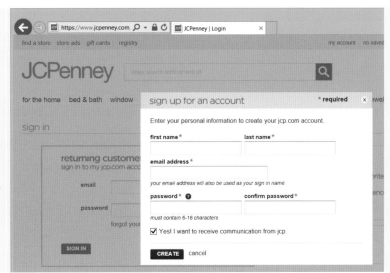

When you pay for purchases, more or less the same rules apply as for online banking. When you create a web account, make sure the web address starts with https://, and check if the padlock appears in the address bar:

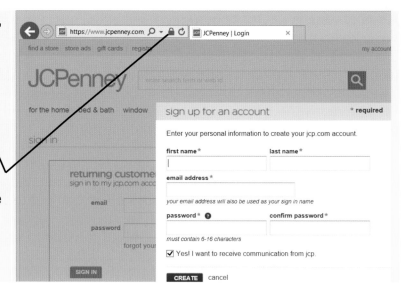

In that case you can be sure the Internet connection to the web page is secure and encrypted and is therefore protected against unauthorized access.

The last important issue is the safety of the payment method you use. Webshops usually offer a variety of payment methods. The most frequently used methods are payments through PayPal or various credit cards.
Each payment method works in a slightly different way and will have their own unique set of risks or security measures, in case things go wrong.

When you checkout, you can often choose between a variety of payment methods.

Many websites will offer information about the payment options on their website:

In the following section you can view a list of various payment methods and the pros and cons of each method.

# 2.10 Safe Online Payment Methods

There is a variety of payment methods used by online retailers from around the world to handle the purchases of goods and services. But what exactly are the advantages and disadvantages of each method? Here we briefly explain what the differences are.

## Bank transfer

A bank transfer means you fill in a transaction form after you have received an invoice. You just follow the instructions on the invoice and decide when to pay the amount. The disadvantage of this method is that many webshops will only process the order after payment has been received and processed. This may cause the delivery time to be longer than with other payment methods.

## One-time only payment authorization

This payment method means you give a one-time only authorization to a webshop or retailer to collect the amount due from your bank account for the purchased item. This authorization is only valid if a printed form has been signed and sent to the webshop in question. This takes quite a lot of time. The order is often only processed after the payment has been processed by the webshop's financial department. That is why very few webshops use this method.

Sometimes, you can authorize such a payment through the Internet. You will need to enter your bank account number on the web page which thereby authorizes the retailer to collect a certain amount from your bank account. This type of automatic payment collection is not legally valid. You will still need to sign and send the authorization form to the retailer to make the payment valid.

If an amount has been unjustly collected through a one-time only payment authorization, you can ask the webshop to withdraw the payment order. If the webshop does not comply, you can block all payments to this webshop through your (online) bank account. Every new withdrawal by this webshop will then be blocked. You can reverse the payment of the amount that has already been withdrawn, usually within eight weeks.

## Credit card

Paying online by credit card always poses a risk. You only need to fill in your 16-digit card number, the name on the card, the expiration date, and the security code (CVC/CID code) in order to pay. This information can all be found on the card itself, and is easy to copy if someone gets a hold of it. That is why *MasterCard* has added the *MasterCard SecureCode* as a means of extra security. This is a personal, secret code you need to enter when you want to pay online.

Credit cards are often used for online payments to foreign webshops. They may have a so-called chargeback policy. You can apply to use this policy if an order has not been delivered; a product appears to be damaged when you receive it; or if you have received the wrong product. The credit card company will claim the amount from the webshop and pay you back. Both PayPal (see below) and the credit card companies lay the burden of proof with the webshop. If the retailer cannot prove he has delivered a certain product, for example, the consumer will always get his money back.

If you still want to pay by credit card, you could use a credit card with a low limit, or a prepaid credit card (see further on in this section).

### PayPal

PayPal was established by the eBay online auction site. It offers consumers and companies an option for paying and receiving money online. It uses an email address associated with your PayPal account to transfer money. Businesses can also transfer money to you. The PayPal account is linked to your bank account or credit card.

A PayPal account provides you with a method for quickly transferring money online, free of charge. Many of the world's largest online retailers offer this payment method. In order to pay, you only need to know the recipient's email address. You just fill in the amount and click Send. The payment will be processed at once and your personal data is never disclosed to the online store.

PayPal also offers protection to its users. In that respect, the PayPal payment method is comparable to using a credit card. If you have purchased a product in an online store and paid for it with PayPal, but have not received the product, PayPal will make sure you get your money back.

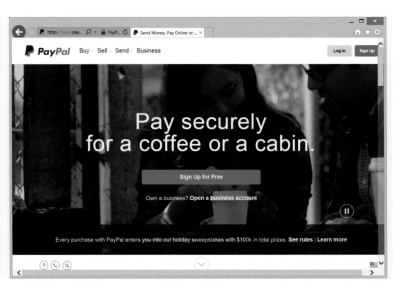

Purchases on eBay will also be reimbursed, usually for the full amount of the purchase. And if you purchase an item that does not match the listed description, you can often get your money back if you file a claim.

## AfterPay

With AfterPay you can pay after the goods have been delivered, through a bank authorization or your bank account, after you have been sent an invoice. More and more webshops are offering AfterPay as a payment method.

AfterPay does not interfere with the delivery process. The webshop itself bears the responsibility of getting their products out to you so that they can be paid as quickly as possible. Some webshops will charge a fee for using AfterPay. And there is a limit to the amount for which you can order items. When you first purchase an item, you will be registered and a maximum amount will be set.

## Cash payments

Some webshops provide an actual address where the goods can be picked up and where you can pay for them in cash or with your bank card. Webshops that also have a 'real' shop often offer this possibility. And if you buy items through second-hand sites or on eBay, you can also agree to pick up the goods in person and pay for them in cash.

## Gift card

Paying with a gift card is becoming increasingly popular. Nowadays, many (web) stores or services issue gift cards that can be bought in supermarkets, newspaper stands, and various other shops.

Examples of these gift cards are the *iTunes* gift cards, the Amazon gift card, and cards for various clothing shops. But you can also buy gift cards for a visit to a beauty parlor, a restaurant and much more.

Paying with a gift card is safe, because you cannot spend more than the amount that is registered to the card. You do not need to spend the entire amount at once.

But you should take into account that the card may be valid for a limited period of time. These cards often expire after a year or within a few years after the last purchase paid with the card.

## Prepaid credit cards

Another safe payment method to use on the Internet is a prepaid credit card. With a prepaid credit card you cannot spend more money than is credited to the card. The card contains a sixteen-digit card number, just like other credit cards, an expiration date, and a security code on the back (CVC/CID code). You need to enter this information when you pay for an item online.

The best-known card is the 3V prepaid Visa card, but there are other cards available from other parties. PayPal even offers its own version: the PayPal Prepaid MasterCard®. You can buy the 3V prepaid Visa card in various supermarkets, newspaper stands, and gas stations for example in Canada and the United Kingdom.

In order to activate the card you will need to create an account. Using the card is not free and there is often a minimum monthly fee required. There may also be additional fees for:

- adding or reloading funds to the card in a shop, or online;
- withdrawing cash with the card;
- payments outside your own country or outside the Eurozone;
- reversing an amount to your bank account;
- inactivity, if you do no use the card for longer than a certain period.

The Paysafe card is another type of prepaid credit card, with which you can pay online and remain anonymous. The card is available at several outlets, such as gas stations, newspaper stands, supermarkets, and tobacconists.
The Paysafe card is available in amounts of 10, 25, 50, or 100 euros or 10, 30, 50, or 100 dollars. You can combine up to ten cards, in order to pay larger amounts.

There are more than 4000 webshops that accept the Paysafe card as a payment method, and websites that offer items such as ringtones and games often accept this card too. The back of the Paysafe card contains a 16-digit PIN code, which will become visible if you scratch the surface of the card. You need to enter this code in the checkout section of the webshop.

When you create an account with My Paysafe card, you can load the PIN codes you have purchased. The total value of all the Paysafe card PIN codes you have loaded represents the amount of money you can use. If you use this method, you will no longer need to enter a 16-digit PIN code. You can use your user name and password for your My Paysafe card account instead.

# 2.11 After You Have Paid

After you have ordered and paid for your product, you will need to wait until it is delivered. Usually, you will receive an email message confirming your purchase order. You can also make a screenshot of the window with the payment data just in case you do not receive a confirmation email right away. To be on the safe side, you can also save a digital or paper copy of each order, order confirmation, and all the terms and conditions.

If you have paid using your online banking account, you will often receive an email confirming your payment. This email is usually sent within a few minutes of placing the order. You can also check your bank account after you have paid.

If there is something wrong with the payment or the receipt, you need to contact your bank, credit card company or webshop at once. If necessary, you can get your money back through chargeback (with a credit card), or a reverse entry (in the case that an automatic payment has been drawn from your bank account). The shop that delivers the product needs to be alerted about this as well.

If you have any complaints concerning the business or the products, the first thing to do is to contact the business in question. Be sure to save all your correspondence with the business. If you cannot reach an agreement, you can always contact the national Consumer Authority in your country (in the USA you need to contact the US Federal Trade Commission, in Australia the ACCC) and lodge a complaint against the webshop.

Another way of handling a complaint about an online retailer is by publishing your story or experiences on a consumer website, such as www.consumeraffairs.com

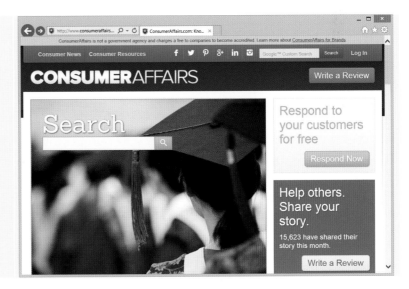

If you publish a complaint on such a website, you need to take into account that these websites only mean to warn and inform the consumers. Publishing a complaint will not guarantee you that the webshop will take your complaint seriously.

## 2.12 Safely Use Facebook, Twitter and Other Social Media

When you use social network sites, such as *Facebook* and *Twitter*, and online discussion forums, the main objective is to share information with others. Lots of people are avid users of these services. But you should try to think in advance about the things you are going to share and the things you really do not want to share. It is very difficult to remove information from the Internet, once it is published. For example, you can publish a photo on your *Facebook* timeline and then remove it again, but if one of your friends has shared this photo with others, your post has been re-used. You will no longer be able to influence it.
If you are using *Facebook*, *Twitter* or some kind of discussion forum, you should follow these rules:

- never share your home address, phone number or email address.
- never tell others when you are going on vacation. There is always a chance that a burglar might notice the message!
- respect each other's privacy. If you do not like your private life to be publicized all over the Internet, others will not like this either. Do you have an awkward picture or a 'funny' story that seems great fun to you, but probably not to the person n question? Then do not publish the photo or story on *Facebook* or one of the other Internet sites.
- if you do not want distant acquaintances to know certain things about you, then do not publish it on *Facebook*.
- If you participate in public discussions on a discussion forum, you can consider using an alias, or just your first name. This way, someone who enters your name in a search engine will not find all your forum posts.

Fortunately, there are a lot of things you can safely share with your followers or friends. Here are some examples:

- a link to a nice web page or video;
- a status update in which you tell what you are currently doing, or what is keeping your mind occupied;
- a series of vacation photos (once you are back home again).

**Tip**

**Others**
Sometimes, you will be amazed at what your friends, acquaintances, or family members want to share through *Facebook* or *Twitter*. Maybe they are not aware that they reveal too much information about themselves, or offend others with their posts or photos. If this is the case, you could try to tell them this, carefully and respectfully.

☞ **Sign in with your *Facebook* account**

Many people do not realize that you can change the *Facebook* privacy settings for each individual message. The setting might be *Everyone*. This means that all other *Facebook* users can see your posts. You can change this:

**Click** 👥 Friends ▼

**Click** ▼ More Options

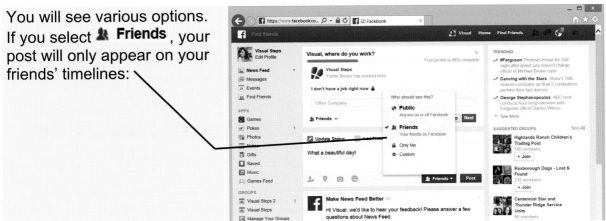

You will see various options. If you select 👥 **Friends**, your post will only appear on your friends' timelines:

*Facebook* will always remember the latest setting and apply it to your new messages. In the *Facebook* settings, you can find a separate *Privacy* section where you can change a number of settings:

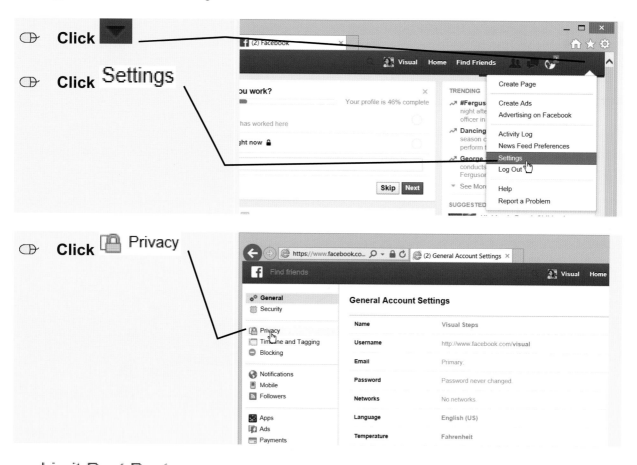

By Limit Past Posts you can adjust the setting for posts you have previously shared with *Everyone* or *Friends of Friends* and change it to *Friends*:

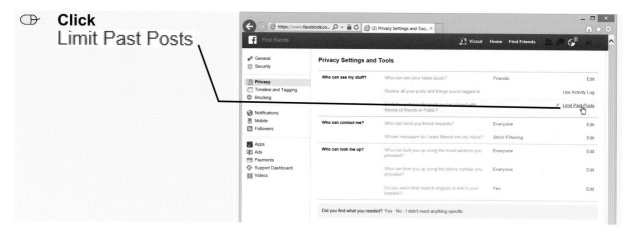

Click **Limit Old Posts**

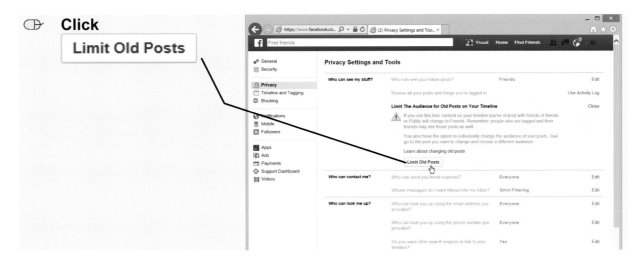

You will need to confirm this change:

Click **Confirm**

Click **Close**

Click **Close**

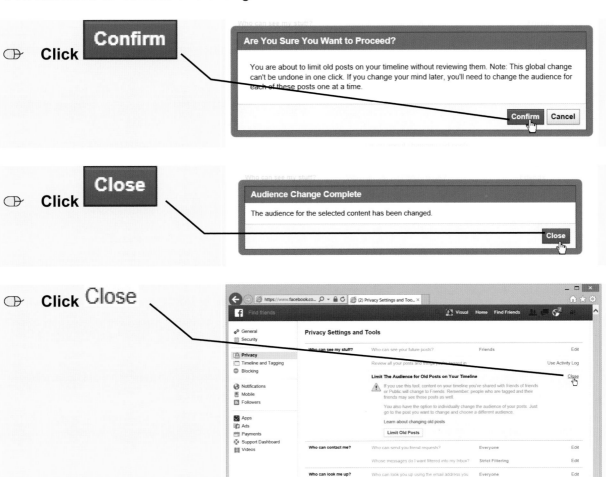

By default, your *Facebook* profile can be found on *Google*. By changing the setting
by ~~Do you want other search engines to link to your timeline?~~, your profile will no longer be
found:

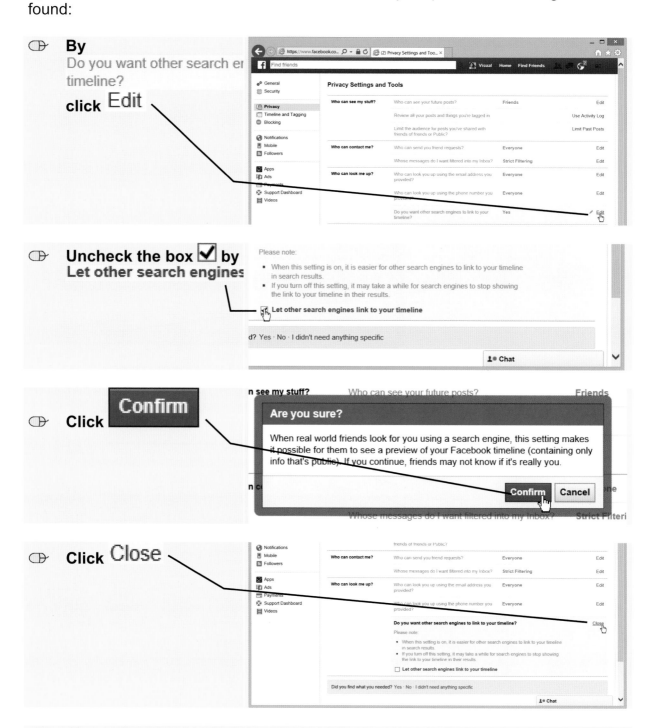

☞ **Sign out with your *Facebook* account**

*Twitter* offers somewhat limited options for protecting your privacy:

### ☞ Sign in with your *Twitter* account

**Click the picture of your *Twitter* account**

**Click** Settings

**Click** Security and privacy

**Drag the scroll box downwards**

Here you can determine who is allowed to tag you in photos published on *Twitter*:

It is possible to protect all your tweets. This means that only followers whom you approve of are allowed to view your tweets:

And you can add a location to your tweets, or not:

Here you can determine whether you want to be found through the email address you have used to sign in with *Twitter*:

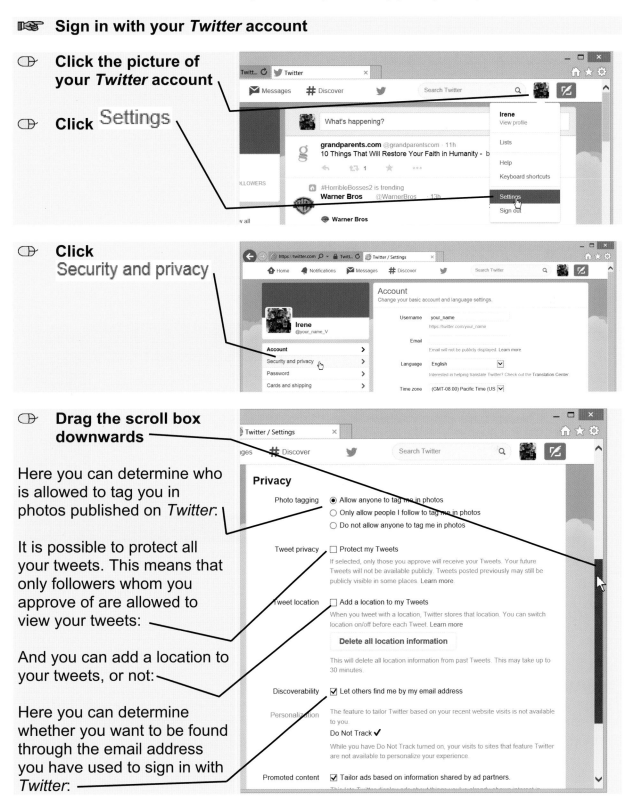

☞ **Drag the scroll box downwards** ————

If you do not want to see any ads based on your interests, then uncheck the box ☑ by Promoted content:

If you have changed any settings:

☞ **Click** Save changes

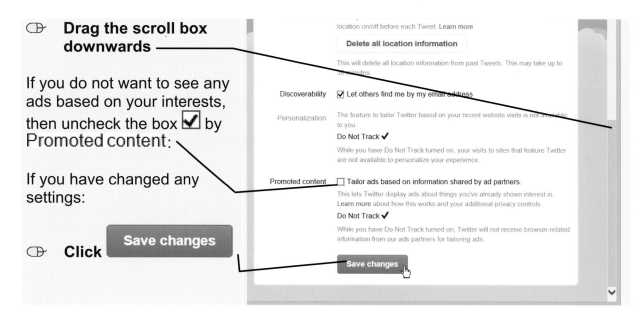

You will need to confirm this by entering your password:

⌨ **Type your password** ——

☞ **Click** Save changes

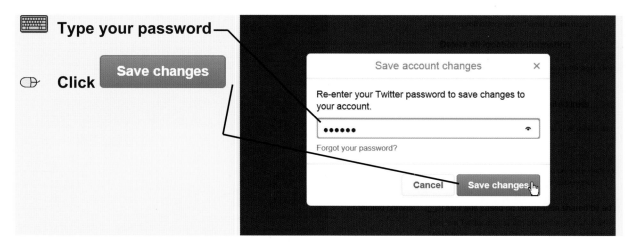

 **Sign out with your *Twitter* account**

 **Close your Internet browser** ✂¹

💡 **Tip**

**Regularly check your Facebook and Twitter settings**
The privacy and account settings for *Facebook* and *Twitter* are regularly updated with new options. It is worthwhile to check these settings on a regular basis, in order to make sure you have used the correct settings for your account.

# 2.13 Background Information

**Dictionary**

| | |
|---|---|
| **Browser history** | The traces you leave on your computer when you surf the Internet. In *Internet Explorer*, the browser history consists of temporary Internet files, cookies, history, data entered in forms, and passwords. |
| **Cookie** | A small text file that is stored on your computer by a website, in order to save certain information. |
| **Hoax** | A sting, swindle, deception, fake story, trick, con. Lots of hoaxes are spread through the Internet. If email is used, it is often in the form of a chain letter. |
| **Https://** | If you see this prefix in front of a web address, the Internet connection is secure (encrypted data traffic). |
| **LastPass** | *LastPass* is a free online service that remembers all the passwords of the websites you are using, within your own account. |
| **Pop-up** | A pop-up is a small window that is displayed on top of the window of the website you are visiting. Pop-ups are usually opened when you visit the first page of a website. They usually contain ads or other promotional items. |
| **Pop-up blocker** | *Pop-up blocking* is an option in *Internet Explorer* that lets you limit or block the displaying of pop-ups. |
| **Spam** | Unsolicited, commercial or mass email. |
| **Spam filter** | Software that discovers spam before it ends up in your *Inbox*. The spam messages are moved to the *Junk email* folder. |
| **Unwanted email** | Unsolicited, mass or commercial email, also known as *spam*. |

*Source: Windows Help and Support, Wikipedia*

## Hoaxes and chain letters

A hoax stands is a deliberately fabricated falsehood made to masquerade as truth. The Internet is full of these hoaxes. When one is used in an email, it is often in the form of a chain letter.

For example, you receive an email message that tells you to forward this message to ten others as soon as possible. If you do not do this, something bad will happen to you or to your loved ones. This is the digital version of the classic chain letter. Other versions contain a sad story, for instance, about someone who is seriously ill, and can only pay for special treatment if the email is forwarded lots of times. Supposedly some kind philanthropist or corporation will then pay one cent for each email that is forwarded. This type of story is rubbish. The sick person does not exist and the photos in the message have probably been plucked from the Internet. If a company decides to help someone, they will never do it like this.

Sometimes these emails contain an 'urgent message' warning you about a dangerous virus on the Internet. They often try to induce you into removing a certain program from your computer. This is usually a program that is essential for the normal working of your computer. If you remove it, you will very likely experience problems with your computer.

If you receive this type of chain letter or hoax, do not forward it. The hoax is primarily intended to gather as many email addresses as possible to be sold or used in future spamming.

Many hoaxes and chain letters are also distributed through *Facebook*:

A very well-known hoax is the message warning you against a new type of (fake) speed camera, used by the police. The recipients of this message are asked to 'behave socially' and share this message with as many others as possible. Many people will actually believe this.

If you would take the time to search for the text of this message on *Google*, you would quickly discover it is a hoax.

*- Continue on the next page -*

In this message you have supposedly won a prize:

You can win this popular gadget by sharing a message and 'liking' a certain web page.

But this page is often not the page from a well-known, legitimate company.

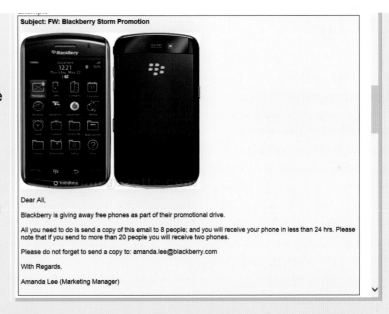

This type of win-a-prize message is usually a scam. The purpose of the scam is to gather as many 'likes' as possible, then empty the page and sell it to others (who think this will become a popular page).

If you know what to look for, you can easily spot a fake 'you have won' message:

- the message is often in English with spelling mistakes;
- the message is not linked to the official website or the official *Facebook* page of the manufacturer;
- the *Facebook* page containing the fake message just contains a single message;
- if the offer appears to be too good to be true, it often is!

Another famous hoax features a picture of a wounded or sick child that is used to induce people to share the message with the claim that '*Facebook* will donate one dollar to a good cause for each shared message'… If *Facebook* intends to donate money they will not do it like this!

Do not share these kinds of *Facebook* messages!

## 2.14 Tips

### Tip

**Blocking pop-ups**

You have surely seen them, those irritating and annoying little windows that suddenly appear while you are surfing the Internet. These are *pop-up* windows. They may be displayed by the website you are currently visiting. But they may also originate from your computer, if it is infected by a previous pop-up window, or by adware or spyware, after you installed a program. In this case, the pop-ups that appear often have nothing to do with the page you are currently viewing.

Some pop-ups are fairly innocent and can easily be closed by clicking ×. Others will open new pop-ups if you close them. The entire pop-up window may also actually be a button. No matter where you click, you will always end up in the next (pop-up) window.

There are also some pop-ups that pose as a dialog box of *Internet Explorer*, for example. They are often in English, so they seem genuine. If you accidentally click the wrong button, they may damage your computer.

If you see a pop-up window:

- Never click the buttons in the pop-up window.
- Do not use the × button to close the pop-up. It is safer to close the pop-up with the key combination Alt and F4.

*Internet Explorer* contains a default pop-up blocker. If a website wants to display a pop-up, it will be blocked automatically. Here you can find the settings for this pop-up blocker:

- **Click** ⚙, Internet options
- **Click the** Privacy **tab**

*- Continue on the next page -*

By default, the pop-up blocker is activated: ————

Because of this pop-up blocker, you may also miss the pop-ups from the regular websites you visit. If you do want to see these pop-ups, you can add them as an exception to the rule:

☞ **Click** Settings

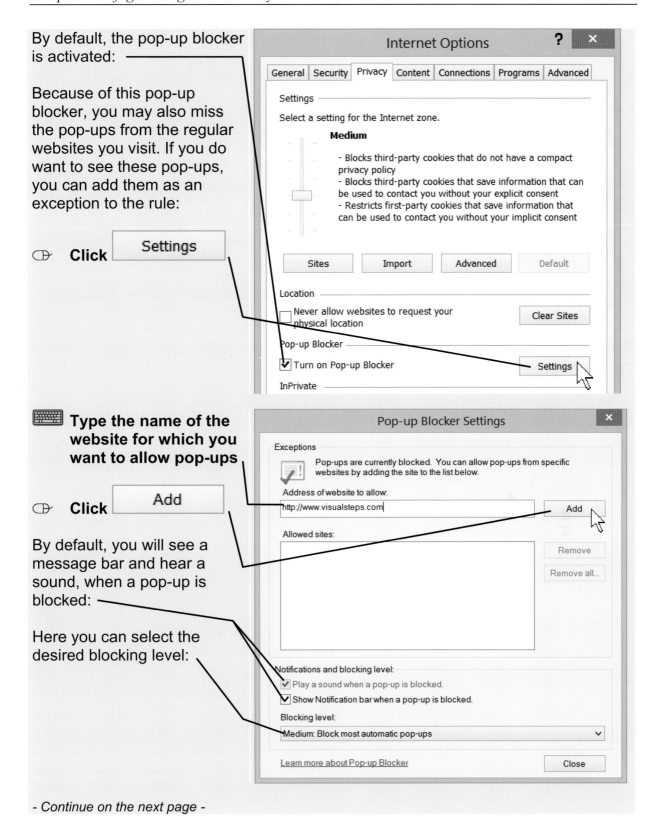

**Type the name of the website for which you want to allow pop-ups**

☞ **Click** Add

By default, you will see a message bar and hear a sound, when a pop-up is blocked:

Here you can select the desired blocking level:

*- Continue on the next page -*

In *Mozilla Firefox*, you can view the pop-up settings in the *Options* window:

☞  **Click** Tools , Options

☞  **Click** Content

By default, pop-ups are
blocked:

Yet you can still allow the
pop-ups on certain websites,
if you wish:

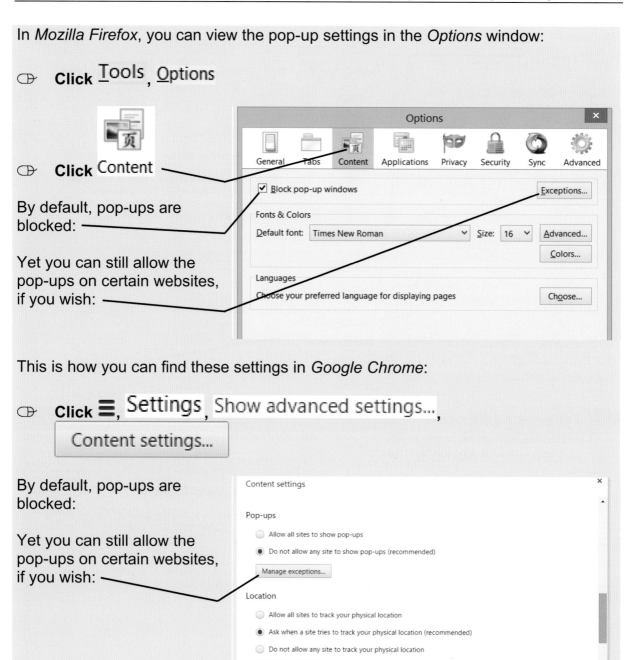

This is how you can find these settings in *Google Chrome*:

☞  **Click** ☰ , Settings , Show advanced settings... ,

Content settings...

By default, pop-ups are
blocked:

Yet you can still allow the
pop-ups on certain websites,
if you wish:

**Tip**

**Searching the Internet**

*Google* is the best-known search engine on the Internet. But there are several other useful websites where you can look for information. Some examples:

- www.bing.com: the search engine powered by *Microsoft*.

- https://startpage.com: an alternative search engine that offers more privacy while you are surfing the web.

- http://www.consumerwatchdog.org: an independent, nonprofit organization, dedicated to the protection of consumers' rights.

- www.pricegrabber.com: a website where you can read and post product reviews, and where prices are compared. Other comparison websites are, among others: www.kelkoo.co.uk, www.shopping.com, www.pricerunner.co.uk, and www.shopzilla.com.

- www.tomshardware.com: an extensive website with a lot of information and reviews on computer hardware such as laptops, tablets, smartphones, etc.

- http://stores.tomshardware.com: here you can compare prices on lots of electronic equipment and other products.

- www.tripadvisor.com: search for reviews by travelers of hotels and vacation accommodation.

- maps.google.com: not only can you plan your trip and get directions, you can also take a closer look at your holiday rental home or hotel on a satellite photo. Just keep in mind that these satellite photos can be several years old.

- www.whitepages.com: search for addresses and phone numbers of persons and businesses in the USA. Most countries will have a phone directory website.

- www.transportdirect.info: Britain's public transport journey planner.

- www.google.com/trustedstores: view reliability of webstores.

**Tip**

**Interpreting search results**

You can find a lot of information on the Internet on all sorts of subjects. But the information you find is not always trustworthy or objective, as anyone can publish their own information. Many businesses will not publish negative comments about their own products. You could compare the information on a company website with what you read in advertisement leaflets. The facts on certain products will surely be accurate, but the products will also be more predominantly promoted.

There are many websites that offer reviews and opinions on products, such as www.pricegrabber.com. This is a website where products are compared and where consumers can post their reviews.

It can be useful to read other consumers' opinions, but keep in mind that these opinions are always highly individual. Reading a review on a subject is not enough to draw the right conclusion. Only when you can read multiple comments, preferably very extensive and supported by good arguments, will you be able to safely draw your own conclusion.

Even an online encyclopedia like *Wikipedia* is compiled by thousands of writers, who are often seduced into mentioning their own opinion on certain topics. Despite the checks performed by the editorial staff, some articles can be subjective, and therefore it is wise to check other sources as well.

In fact, on the Internet you should behave a bit like a journalist who is getting his information from different sources. If you want to get an idea of how trustworthy a website is, you should really check who has published the info on this website. You can often find a link called *About Us* or *Who are We?* that provides information on the creators of the website and explains the reasons for creating it.

**Tip**

**Wi-Fi**

Accessing the Internet while connected to Wi-Fi has become increasingly popular. You can set up and use a wireless Wi-Fi network yourself at home. You can also access Wi-Fi in lots of other places, such as restaurants, shops, hotels and even in the train. This is often free of charge, but sometimes you have to pay for it.

A public Wi-Fi connection outside of the home is not always secure, which means it can be used by anyone, also by hackers who want to hijack the Internet. Criminals can use these public networks to take a look at your activities on the Internet, and may be able to steal your passwords for example, if you use your laptop for your banking transactions. This will not happen right away, of course, but it is important that you are aware of the risks.

Taking a quick look at a favorite website at the train station, or in a hotel, is not a problem, but we advise against using a public Wi-Fi for banking transactions or shopping online. It is safer to connect to the Internet through a mobile data network (3G/4G). You can buy a hardware lock or a USB connection stick for your computer, for this purpose. This device contains a SIM card. You just need to insert it into your computer or laptop.

If you notice any strange events while you are surfing the Internet, you should always break the connection immediately.

At home it is equally important to secure your Wi-Fi network by using a password. Otherwise, the neighbors may also 'borrow' your Internet connection, or even hack into your computer or tablet. When you are setting up the Internet connection you are often asked to enter a password, and you can do this in just a few simple steps. There is a big chance that your Wi-Fi network is already password-protected.

If your wireless Internet connection is not already secured with a password, you can read the manual that came with your modem or router, or check your Internet provider's website, and find out how to set a password for it.

**Tip**

**Protecting your user account with a password**
On your computer you may have important, personal or legal documents stored that you do not want others to see or edit. This is why it is recommended to set up a password for your computer.
In *Windows*, every user has their own user account, on principle. If any other user, your child or grandchild, for example, wants to use your computer, you will need to let him or her log on with another account. Regarding children, it is best to grant them limited user rights, so they will not be able to install programs without your permission, for instance. In the *Control Panel* you can view the settings for the user accounts on your computer:

☞ **Open the *Control Panel* ❨❩³**

⊕ **Click** User Accounts and Family Safety , User Accounts ,
🛡 Manage another account

⊕ **Click the account**

⊕ **Click** Create a password

⌨ **Type the desired password** ——————

⌨ **Re-type the password**

You can also add a password reminder, if you wish: but make sure that others will not be able to use this to decipher or discover your password. ——————

If you have finished:

⊕ **Click**
Create password

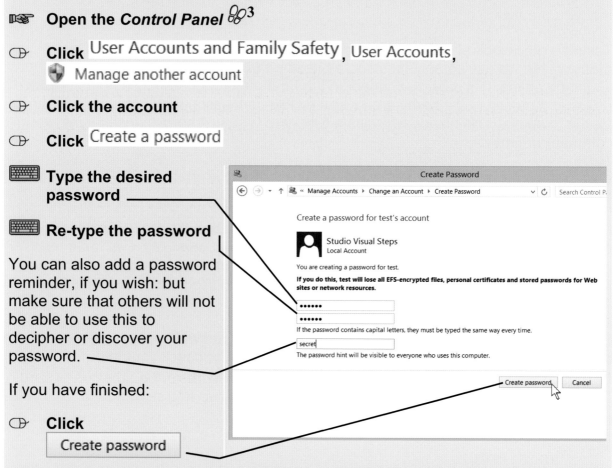

Make sure that all the accounts on the computer are password-protected, and that you have set up your own account with Administrator rights. You can also grant these rights to users that are allowed to view your files. The other users should get a Default (Standard) type of account. If you do not do this, other users will still be able to view your files in their user account (through a workaround). You can change the account type with the Change the account type option.

# 3. Creating Backups

If your computer contains photos, legal documents, or other files of vital importance, it is essential that you back these up on a regular basis. In this way, you will always have a copy of this data in case something happens to your computer. You may experience a malfunction, an infection by malware, a fire, theft, short-circuiting, or even an accidental deletion of your own which triggers the loss of data.

The *Windows* backup program has several options for creating backups. You can create a backup of the entire hard drive and all its settings for example, or just a backup of important, personal files.

In the past, backups were stored on floppy disks, CDs, or DVDs. These types of storage media had one big disadvantage, you could not save a lot of information on them. Larger backups soon required multiple disks, CDs, or DVDs. Since the arrival of the *external hard drive* everything has changed. Nowadays, you can also save your backups online, in the *cloud*.

You can use *restore points* to restore the *Windows* settings to a previous state, in case you experience problems with the stability of your computer.

In this chapter you will learn how to:

- create a backup copy;
- restore a backup;
- create restore points and restore them.

 **Please note:**

You can save a backup on DVDs, USB sticks, memory cards or on an external hard drive. In this chapter you will learn how to create a backup and store it on an external hard drive.

 **Please note:**

If you want to back up a laptop, it is recommended that you connect the laptop to a power outlet. Do not rely on battery power alone. This will ensure that the backup operation is not thwarted by a low battery level.

**Please note:**

If you want to restore your data, in case of a fire or theft of your computer, it is essential that you keep your backup files in a different physical place other than your computer. Give the backup drive to a friend or family member, for safekeeping.

 **Please note:**

Creating and restoring backups and restore points is slightly different in *Windows 8.1* and *Windows 7*. That is why we have split the actions needed for *Windows 8.1* and *Windows 7* into different sections. If you are using *Windows 7*, you can skip to *section 3.8 Which Type of Backup in Windows 7?* on page 146.

# 3.1 Which Type of Backup in Windows 8.1?

You can secure your data by creating backups, but also by manually copying data to another drive or other storage media. The option you choose, depends on the type of data, and the way in which you want to use it.

The following options will help you decide which backup method to choose:

| I want to…                                                                              | section |
|-----------------------------------------------------------------------------------------|---------|
| • create a manual backup of my personal files.                                          | 3.2     |
| • let *Windows* create automatic backups at fixed points in time, so I do not have to bother with this myself. | 3.2     |
| • restore a backup of my personal files to the computer.                                | 3.3     |
| • create a full backup (system backup) of all the programs, files, and settings.        | 3.4     |
| • secure personal files, but use them separately, on other computers, and be able to restore them one by one. | 3.5     |
| • save *Windows* settings as a restore point.                                           | 3.6     |
| • restore *Windows* settings using a restore point.                                     | 3.7     |

You will usually want to create a backup for safety reasons. But it is also a good idea to create one when you have a very large number of files. When you create a backup, all the files are compressed into a single file. This means the files will take up much less space than if you were to copy them in the regular manner. But you will need a backup program to restore these files before using them again.

If it just concerns a few separate files, you can manually copy them to a USB stick or an external hard drive using *Windows Explorer*. You can then open and edit the files directly from these devices, if necessary.
You can decide which method best suits your needs or requirements.

# 3.2 Backing Up Your Personal Files in Windows 8.1

In *Windows 8.1* you can create a backup of your own files. This is one way of securing important data in case something happens to your computer.

☞ **If necessary, connect the external hard drive to your computer**

 **Please note:**

Your external hard drive may not have enough free space to store a system copy. If this is the case, you will see a warning. You will need to have another external hard drive on hand.

☞ **Go to the Start screen** $\mathcal{O}\!\mathcal{O}^2$

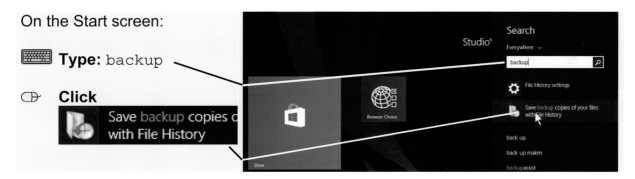

On the Start screen:

⌨ **Type:** backup

🖰 **Click**

    Save backup copies with File History

You will see the *File History* window:

Select the drive where you will back up your files:

🖰 **Click** Select drive

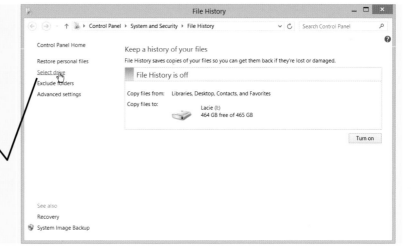

**Click the external hard drive**

**Please note:** this should not be one of the drives of your own computer.

At the bottom of the window:

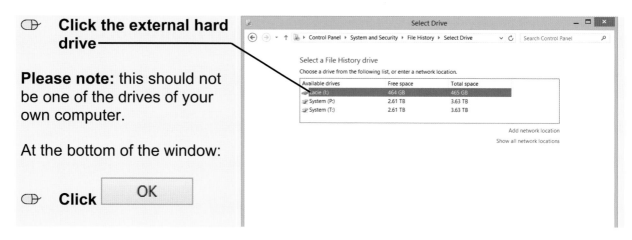

 **Click** OK

---

💡 **Tip**
**The name of the external hard drive**
*Windows* will usually recognize the external hard drive by its brand name.

---

You may still need to turn on the file history option:

 **If necessary, click**
Turn on

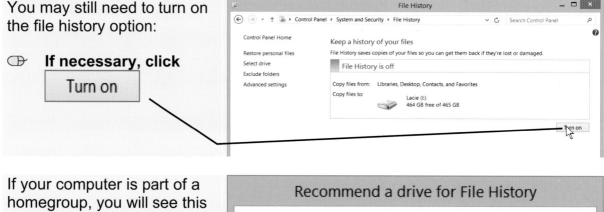

---

If your computer is part of a homegroup, you will see this window if you are using the function for the first time:

 **If necessary, click**
No

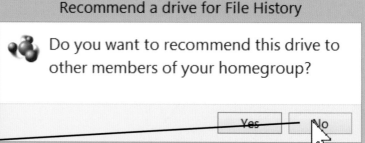

Recommend a drive for File History

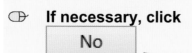 Do you want to recommend this drive to other members of your homegroup?

Yes    No

---

 **Please note:**
The file history that is set applies to the current user only. Each user will need to set up his or her own file history.

A backup is made at once. When a backup process has finished, you will see Run now:

If you do not want to create a backup of all the folders:

☞ **Click** Exclude folders

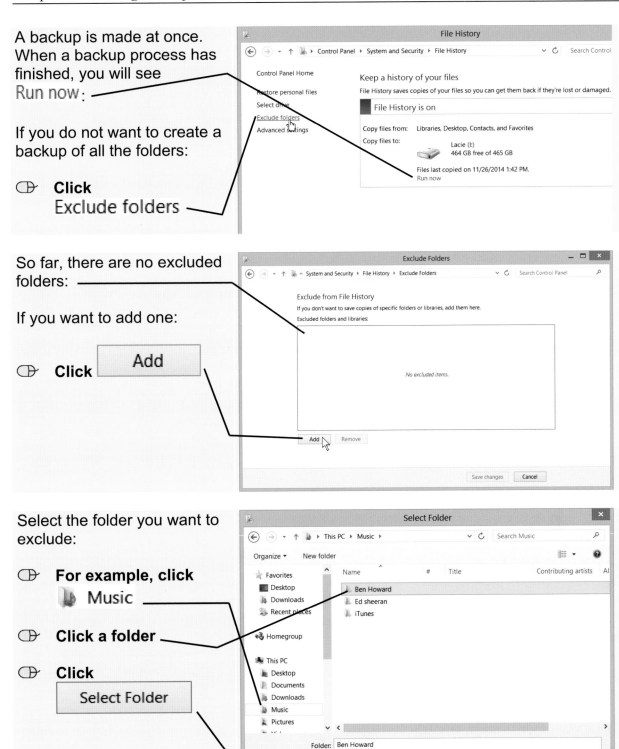

So far, there are no excluded folders:

If you want to add one:

☞ **Click** Add

Select the folder you want to exclude:

☞ **For example, click** Music

☞ **Click a folder**

☞ **Click** Select Folder

You will see the folder that is excluded:

You can exclude more folders, if you wish.

⊕ **Click** Save changes

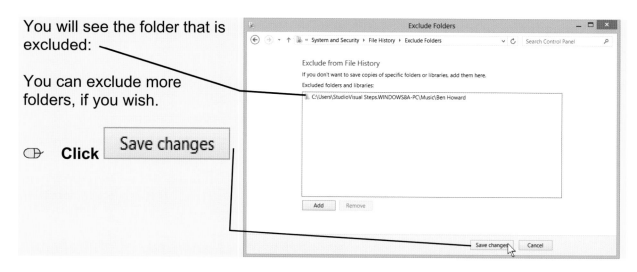

If desired, you can adjust even more settings for creating backups:

⊕ **Click** Advanced settings

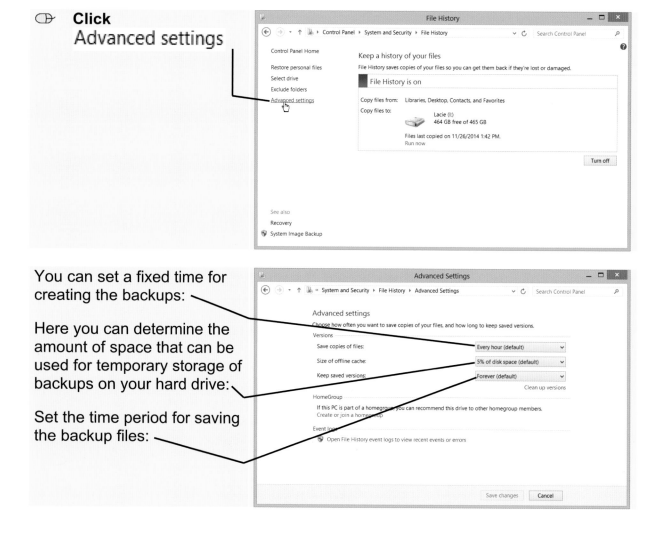

You can set a fixed time for creating the backups:

Here you can determine the amount of space that can be used for temporary storage of backups on your hard drive:

Set the time period for saving the backup files:

In order to free up space on your backup drive, you can delete older backups:

☞ **Click**

Clean up versions

In this example, you could delete the backups that are more than one year old:

You can select a different time period, if you wish.

In this example we will not delete the backups:

☞ **Click** Cancel

If you have changed any settings, be sure to click Save changes.

Nothing has changed in this example:

☞ **Click** Cancel

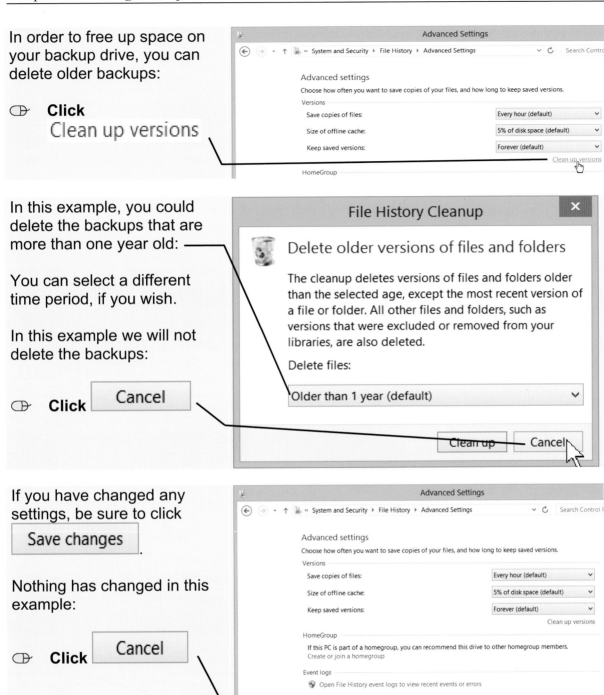

You can update the backup files manually, if you have edited or added any important new files:

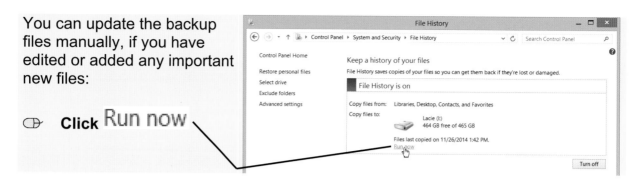

 **Click** Run now

In future, the backups will be created automatically according to the preferences you have set.

## 🖐 **Please note:**

In this example, an hourly backup is created of all files that have changed. This is called an *incremental backup*. This means that the entire hard drive is not backed up every time, just the changes. You can change the time period to twice a week, for example, if you wish. If the files on your computer do not change very often, you will not need to create a backup every hour.

## 🖐 **Please note:**

The backup can only be made if the backup destination (the external hard drive) is connected and available. If the backup destination is not available, a temporary backup will be stored on your computer's hard drive.

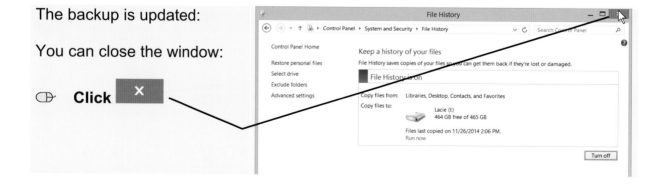

 **Click** Close

The backup is updated:

You can close the window:

 **Click** ✕

# 3.3 Restoring Personal Files

You also need to use the backup program when you want to restore personal files. You can open a window directly and then select the library or files to be restored:

 **Go to the Start screen** $\mathscr{O}\mathscr{O}^2$

⌨️ **Type:** restore

👆 **Click**

In this example, the *Music* folder contains the files that have been backed up:

Select the library you want to restore:

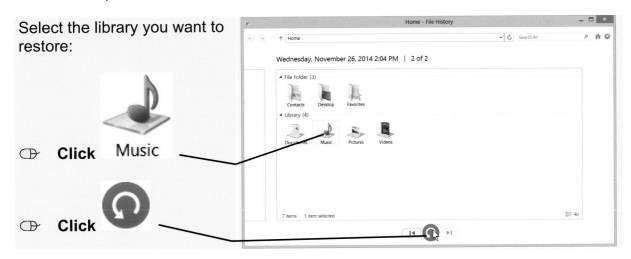

👆 **Click** Music

👆 **Click**

💡 **Tip**
**Restore an older version**
By default, the most recent version will be restored. In order to restore an older version:

👆 **At the bottom of the window, click** ◀|

💡 **Tip**
**Restoring multiple folders**
If you want to restore multiple folders or libraries, you can select them by pressing

and holding **Ctrl** or **Shift** down while you select the folders and files.

To replace all the files on the computer that have the same name:

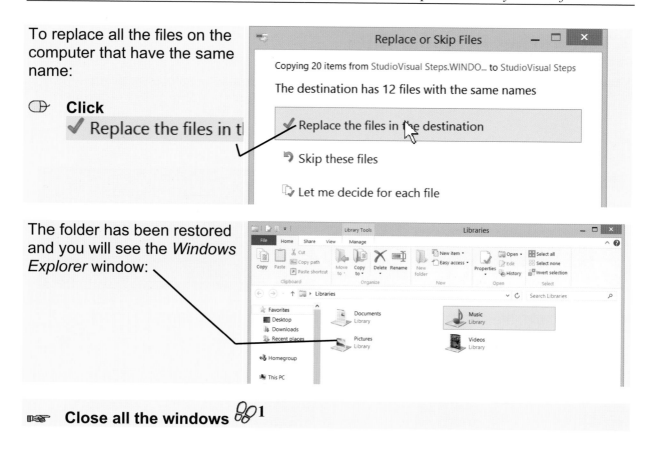

⊕ **Click**

✓ Replace the files in t|

The folder has been restored and you will see the *Windows Explorer* window:

☞ **Close all the windows** 1

# 3.4 Creating a System Image

You can also create a full backup in *Windows 8.1*. This type of backup is called a *system image* or *system copy*. A system image contains copies of your programs, system settings and files. You can use a system image to restore the full content of your computer, in the case of a hard drive crash or if the computer stops working for other reasons.

## ➲ Please note:

You cannot use the same external hard drive for saving both the file history and a system image. If you try to do this, you will see an error message.

If your external hard drive does not have enough free space for a system image, you will see a warning message. You will need to use a different external hard drive with more memory.

Your hard drive also needs to be formatted for the NTFS file system. Usually, NTFS is already the default formatting method for the external hard drive. You can find more information about this in *Windows Help and Support*, or in the manual that came with the external hard drive.

**Please note:**

If you want to restore a full system image, you may need to use a USB restore drive. In *Windows Help and Support* you can also read more about this tool.

 **Please note:**

Creating a full system image may take several hours. We suggest you read through this section first, and then perform the actions as described if you really want to create a system image.

You will be creating a system image on a different hard drive:

☞ **If necessary, connect the external hard drive to your computer**

☞ **Open the *File History* window** 🐾**13**

In the bottom left corner of the window:

☞ **Click**
🛡 System Image Backup

See also

Recovery

System Image Backup

You will see the *Create a system image* window:

First, the program will check which devices have been connected and are suitable for storing this backup copy:

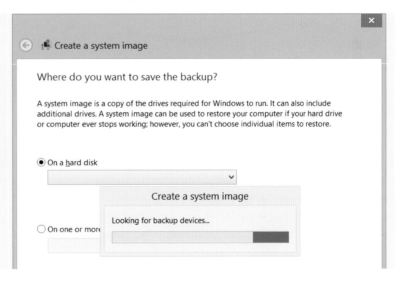

You choose the destination where the system image will be saved. This can be an external hard drive or a DVD:

 **By** On a hard disk,

click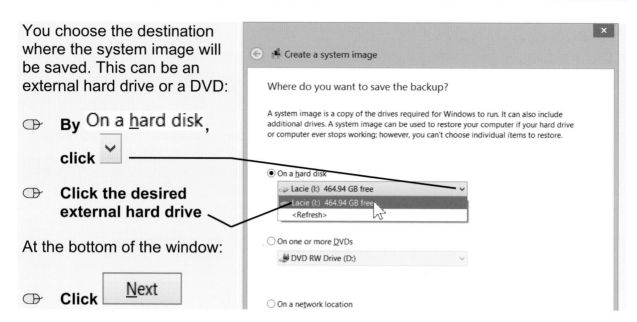

 **Click the desired external hard drive**

At the bottom of the window:

 **Click** Next

## HELP! The drive is not suitable.

If you want to create a system image, your hard drive needs to be formatted for the NTFS file system. Usually, NTFS is already the default format. You can find more information about this in *Windows Help and Support*, or in the manual that came with the external hard drive.

If the drive has been formatted incorrectly, you will see a message:

If you have multiple drives, you can indicate which drives are to be included in the system backup:

By default, the hard drive that contains the *Windows* operating system is already selected:

 **Check the box ☑ by the hard drives you want to include**

You will see the required and the available space:

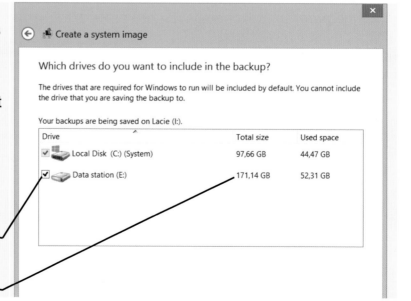

At the bottom of the window:

Click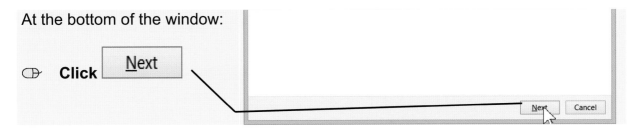

You will see a summary of the backup data:

If you want to create the backup copy:

Click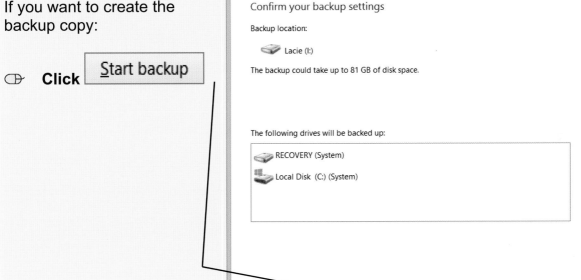

While the system image is made, you will see this window:

Creating a system image may take several hours and the process should not be interrupted. If the backup operation stops, you will need to start again.

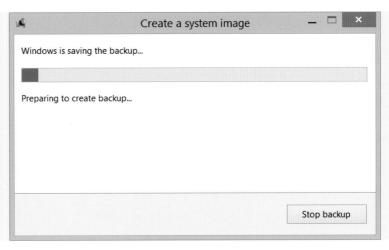

Once the backup is created:

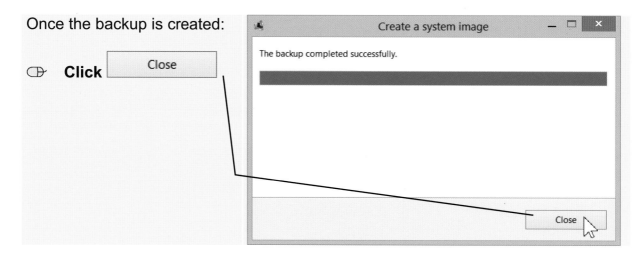

 **Click**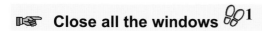

When the backup has been made, you will have an external hard drive that contains a full copy of your current system. Store this backup copy in a safe place.

 **Close all the windows** $\mathscr{C}$1

💡 **Tip**

**Regularly create system images**

It is recommended that you create these system images on a regular basis. This way, you always have the most recent copy of your hard drive at your disposal.

👉 **Please note:**

If you need to restore the computer by using the system image, the entire system will be restored. It is not possible to restore individual files. All current programs, system settings, and files will be replaced.
This means it is important to create regular backups, in order to secure the files you have recently added or edited.

👉 **Please note:**

If you want to restore a system image, you will need to use the DVD with the *Windows* operating system. If you do not have this DVD, you can sometimes create a so-called system recovery disc in *Windows 8.1*, through an auxiliary program that has been supplied by the computer manufacturer. In *Windows 7* you can create a system recovery disc by clicking 🛡️ Create a system repair disc in the *Backup and Restore* window.

# 3.5 Copying Personal Files to an External Hard Drive

You do not need to do a full backup if you want to make a safety copy of one or more files. If there are not too many files involved, and they are not too big, and you want to use these files elsewhere (on other computers), you can copy these files onto an external hard drive in the usual way. You can do this in the *Explorer* window.

☞ **If necessary, connect the external hard drive to your computer**

☞ **Open *Windows Explorer* 🦶14**

☞ **Open the folder with the file you want to copy**

⏏ **Click the file**

⏏ **Right-click the file**

⏏ **Click Send to**

⏏ **Click the external hard drive**

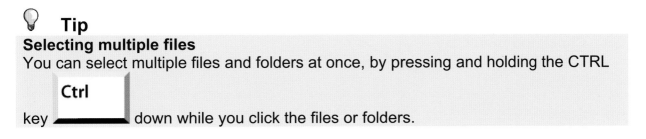

The file is copied to the external hard drive.

💡 **Tip**

**Selecting multiple files**
You can select multiple files and folders at once, by pressing and holding the CTRL

**Ctrl**

key ▬▬▬ down while you click the files or folders.

## HELP! The file already exists.

If the external hard drive contains a file with the same name, you will see the window below:

In *Windows 8.1*:

Replace the file on the hard drive by the file that is to be copied: ─────────

Do not copy the file: ─────

Compare the file and if necessary copy it and give it a different name: ────

☞ **Click the desired option** ──────

If you select
🗋 Compare info for both files
in *Windows 8.1*, you will see this window:

In order to leave the file in the destination folder unchanged and copy the new file to a file name with a digit added to the name:

☞ **Check the box ☑ by both files** ────

☞ **Click** [ Continue ] ─────

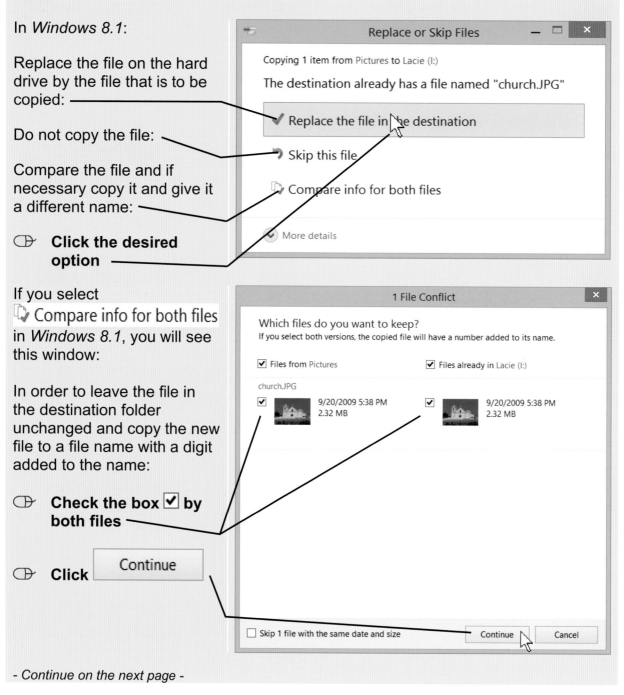

- *Continue on the next page -*

In *Windows 7*:

Replace the file on the hard drive by the file that is to be copied:

Do not copy the file:

Copy the file, but with a different name:

☞ **Click the desired option**

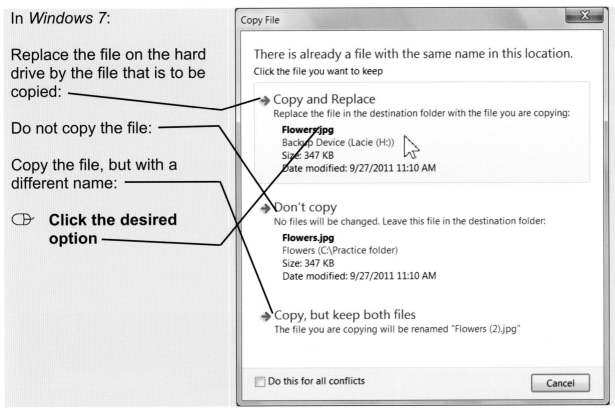

---

Tip

**Restore a folder**
You can restore a folder in the same way. You can select multiple files and folders at once by pressing and holding the CTRL key 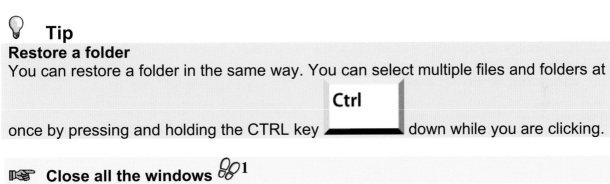 down while you are clicking.

☞ **Close all the windows** 📖¹

# 3.6 Creating Restore Points

There can always come a day when *Windows 8.1* suddenly stops working. This may happen for instance, after installing a new program. If the problem solving tools have not helped you, you can use the *System Restore* function.
You can restore your computer to an earlier state, that is to say, a certain restore point. You can select a date when you know that *Windows* was working normally. This restore point is a reflection of the status of the stored system files on the computer at that time.

## Please note:

Restore points will only save changes in the operating system and in certain application files. If you restore the system to a previous state by using a restore point, this will not affect your personal data files. Your text files, email messages, photos, etc. will not be changed.
This means you cannot use restore points to undo the deletion of a document, email or photo.

*Windows 8.1* creates restore points every day, and also on important occasions, such as the installation of new programs or devices.
If necessary, you can create a restore point manually. You can do this before you introduce a new device (such as a printer/scanner), install an update or make other changes to a program. To create a restore point:

☞ **Go to the Start screen** 🦶2

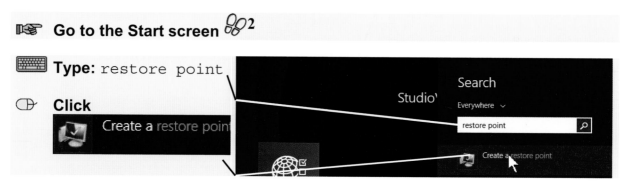

⌨ **Type:** restore point

👆 **Click**

Create a restore point

You will see the *System Protection* tab in the *System Properties* window:

👆 **Click the C: drive**

In most cases, this will be the drive where *Windows 8.1* has been installed.

👆 **Click**

Create...

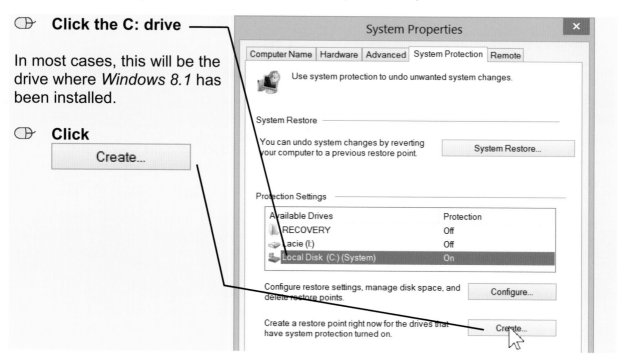

Enter an identifiable name for the new restore point:

 **Type:** Practice
restore point

☞ **Click** [ Create ]

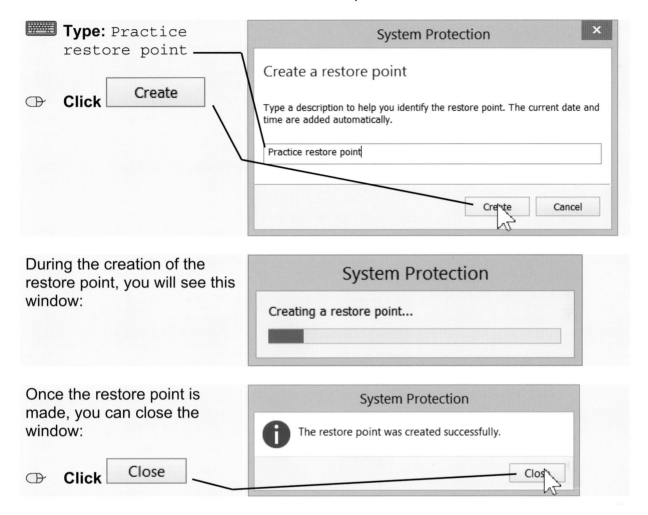

During the creation of the restore point, you will see this window:

Once the restore point is made, you can close the window:

☞ **Click** [ Close ]

# 3.7 Reverting to a Restore Point

If you experience problems with the system, after an update or after you have installed a device, you can revert the system to a restore point as follows:

## 🐾 Please note:

If you use *System Recovery*, the computer will be re-started. So you need to close all your programs and save your work first, before you start using *System Recovery*.

☞ **If necessary, open the *System Properties* window** 🐾[15]

**Click**

**System Restore...**

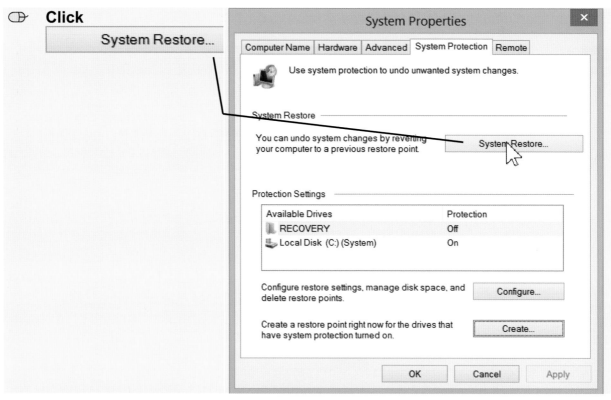

After a short while, the *System Recovery* program will open:

In this example we have selected the restore point we previously created:

**Click**   **Next >**

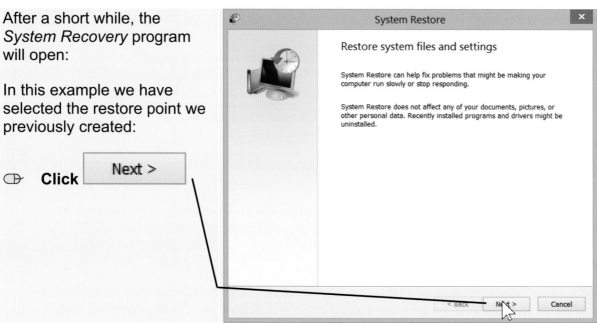

**Click**
Practice restore point

First, you can check whether
reverting to a restore point
will have any effect on your
programs and drivers:

 **Click**

Scan for affected progra

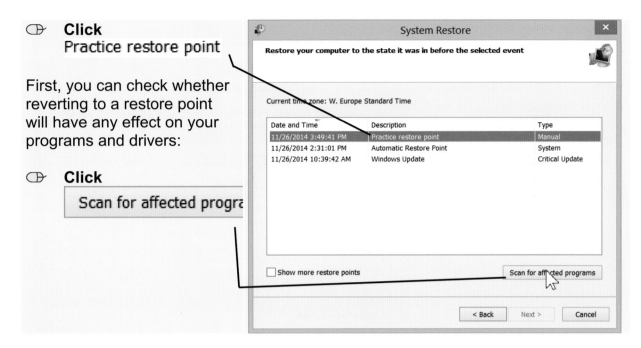

 **Please note:**

By default, only the restore points for the previous five days are displayed. If your
problem has existed for a longer period of time, for example, since you installed a
printer a week ago, you can check the box ✔ by **Show more restore points** to
display older restore points.

 **Please note:**

In this example you will see a single drive, but this may be different on your own
computer. In any case, you should restore the drive that contains the *Windows*
operating system. In most cases, this is the C: drive.

The programs and drivers are
checked:

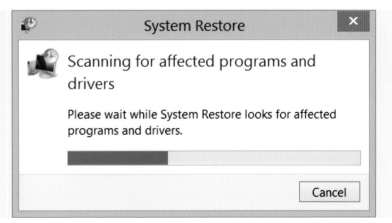

In this example, no problems have been found:

At the bottom of the window:

 **Click** Close

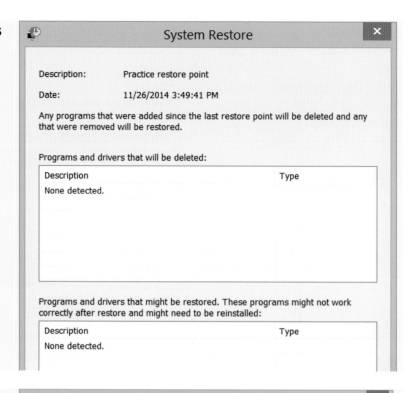

If there are no problems, you can continue:

 **Click** Next >

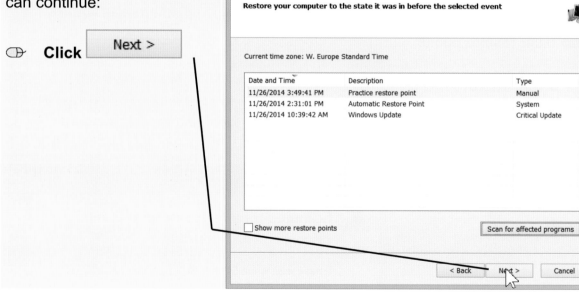

## HELP! Problems have been found.

If any problems have been found on your computer, you can stop the restore operation by clicking [ Cancel ]. Then, you need to check whether you should take any other measures before restoring the system. For example, if it is easy to re-install a certain program afterwards, you could decide to go ahead and restore the system anyway.

☞ **Click the desired drive, if you wish**

In this example you will see a single drive, but this may be different on your own computer.
At any rate, you will need to restore the drive that contains the installation of *Windows 8.1*. In most cases, this is the C: drive.

☞ **Click** [ Finish ]

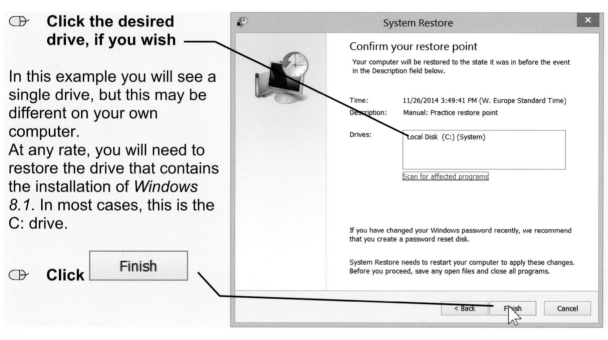

You will be asked to confirm this operation:

☞ **Click** [ Yes ]

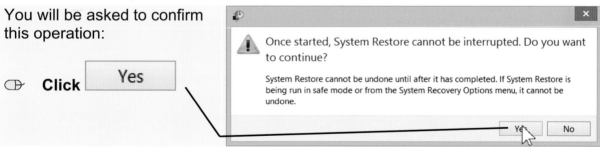

While the system files are being restored, you will see this window:

Once the system has been restored, *Windows 8.1* will be closed and the computer will be restarted. When you see your desktop again, you will see this message:

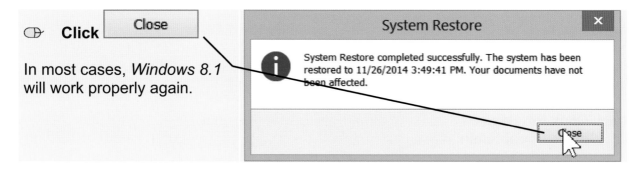

You can continue reading with the *Background Information*:

☞  **Continue on page 160**

# 3.8 Which Type of Backup in Windows 7?

You can secure your data by creating backups, as well as copying data to another drive yourself. What is best, depends on the type of data and the way in which you want to use it.
The following options will help you decide which backup method to choose:

| I want to… | section |
|---|---|
| • create a manual backup of personal files. | 3.9 |
| • let *Windows* create automatic backups at fixed time intervals, so I no longer need to bother with this. | 3.9 |
| • restore a (manual) backup of personal files to the computer. | 3.10 |
| • create a full system copy (system image) of all the programs, files, and settings. | 3.11 |
| • secure personal files, but I want to be able to use them individually, and restore them one by one. | 3.12 |
| • save the *Windows* settings as a restore point. | 3.13 |
| • restore Windows settings using a restore point. | 3.14 |

You will usually want to create a backup for safety reasons. But it is also a good idea to create one when you have a very large number of files. When you create a backup, all the files are compressed into a single file. This means the files will take up much less space than if you were to copy them in the regular manner. But you will need a backup program to restore these files before using them again.

If it just concerns a few separate files, you can manually copy them to a USB stick or an external hard drive using *Windows Explorer*. You can then open and edit the files directly from these devices, if necessary.
You can decide which method works best for you.

# 3.9 Creating a Backup of Personal Files

In *Windows 7* you can create a backup copy of your own files. This is one way of securing important data in case something happens to your computer.

☞ **If necessary, connect the external hard drive to your computer**

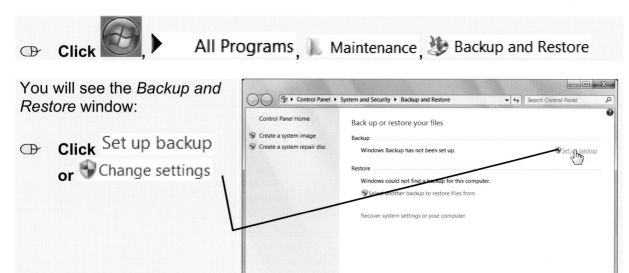

☞ **Click** , ▶ All Programs , Maintenance , Backup and Restore

You will see the *Backup and Restore* window:

☞ **Click** Set up backup

or 🛡Change settings

Now you can choose the backup destination:

☞ **Click the desired drive**

At the bottom of the window:

☞ **Click** Next

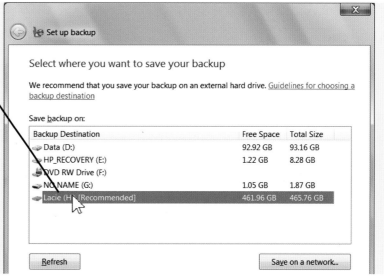

You can choose which type of backup you want to create:

A backup of important files:

For more information, click
How does Windows choose wha

You can also choose which files you want to save:

 **Click the radio button by** Let me choose

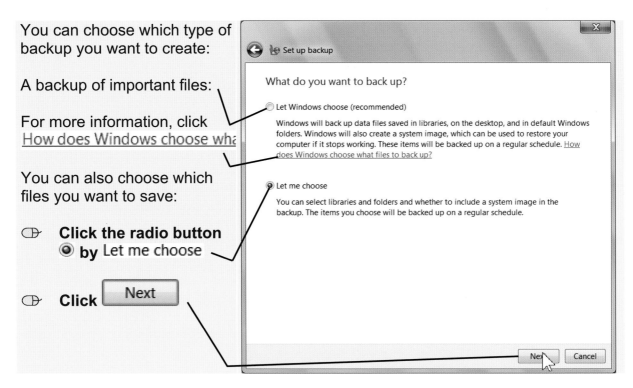

◉ **Click** Next

💡 **Tip**

### Let Windows perform the backup procedure
You can let *Windows* do the work and perform the backup procedure for the most important files. An automatic backup will be created of the libraries, contacts, and favorites, among other items.

◉ **Click the radio button by** Let Windows choose (re

At the bottom of the window:

◉ **Click** Next

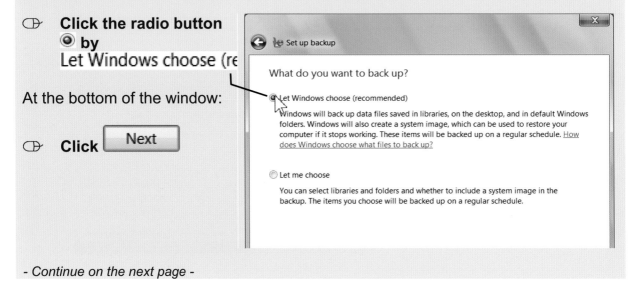

*- Continue on the next page -*

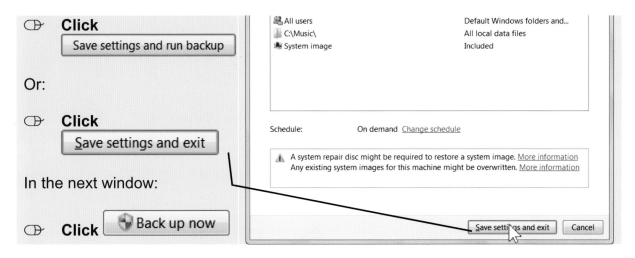

⊙ **Click**
Save settings and run backup

Or:

⊙ **Click**
S̲ave settings and exit

In the next window:

⊙ **Click** ⊕ Back up now

Now you can select the folders you want to include in the backup:

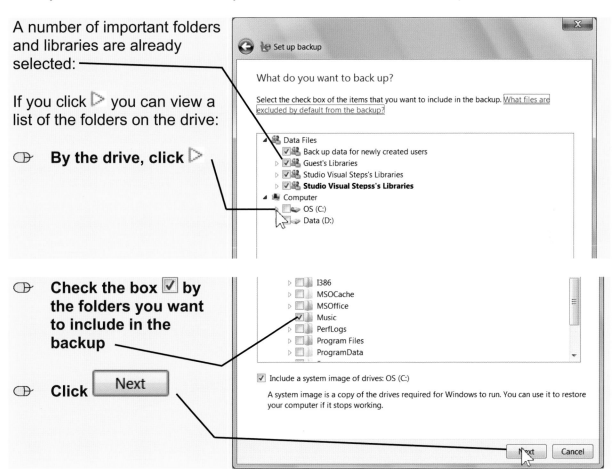

A number of important folders and libraries are already selected:

If you click ▷ you can view a list of the folders on the drive:

⊙ **By the drive, click** ▷

⊙ **Check the box ☑ by the folders you want to include in the backup**

⊙ **Click** Next

You will see a summary of the backup settings:

The backup is automatically set to run at a certain time:

You can change that:

☞ **Click**
  Change schedule

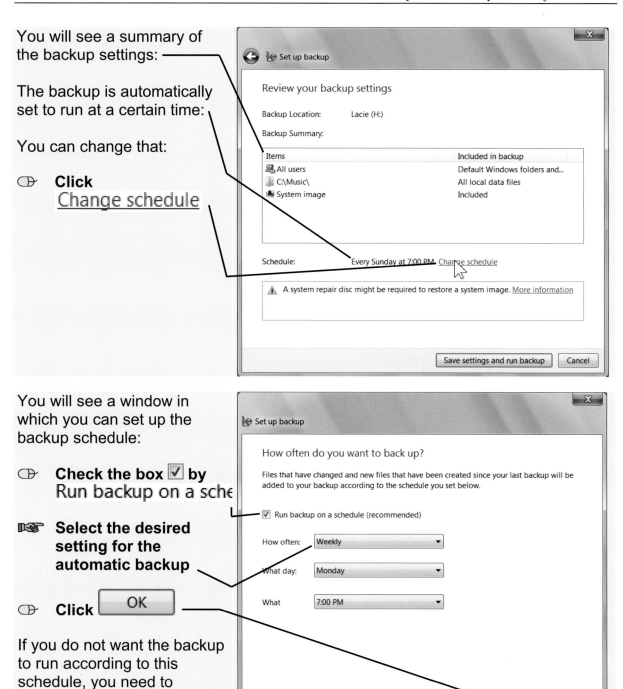

You will see a window in which you can set up the backup schedule:

☞ **Check the box ☑ by**
  Run backup on a sche

☞ **Select the desired setting for the automatic backup**

☞ **Click** OK

If you do not want the backup to run according to this schedule, you need to uncheck the box ☑ by
Run backup on a schedule (recon

An automatic backup will be created at the time you have indicated. If the computer is turned off at that time, the backup will be created as soon as the computer is turned on again and the external hard drive is available.

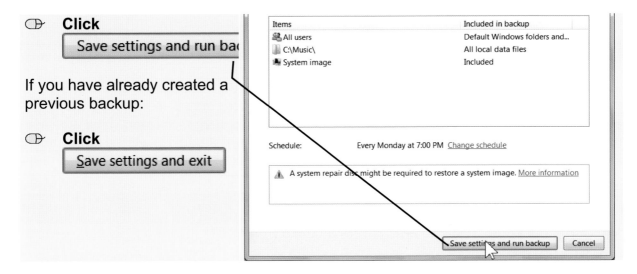

☞ **Click**

> Save settings and run ba◁

If you have already created a previous backup:

☞ **Click**

> S̲ave settings and exit

If you have already created a previous backup, you will see the *Backup and Restore* window first:

☞ **Click**

> 🛡 Back up now

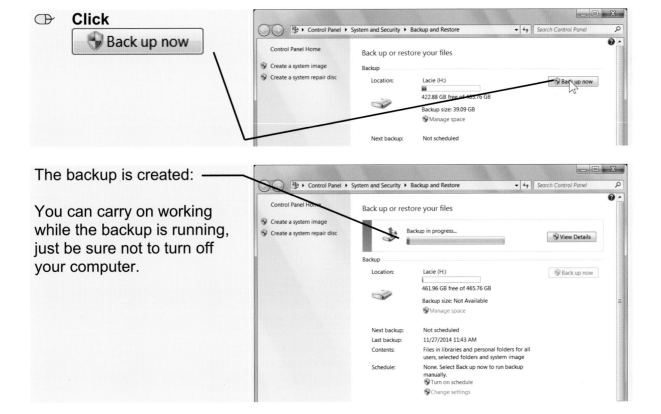

The backup is created:

You can carry on working while the backup is running, just be sure not to turn off your computer.

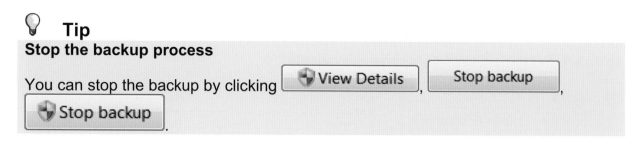

**Tip**

**Stop the backup process**

You can stop the backup by clicking View Details, Stop backup,
Stop backup.

The first time you create a backup, all the data you have chosen to be saved will be included in the backup. The next time, and all subsequent times, the backup will only include the data that has changed since the last backup was performed. This is called an incremental (additional) backup. This incremental backup will be added to the external hard drive. This saves a lot of time and disk space.

The *Windows 7* backup program will automatically create incremental backups of changed data only, after the first full backup has been made, if a schedule has been set for the backups. You can also create a backup manually, by clicking  Back up now. For example, if you have made changes or added important files.

**Please note:**

The options you selected when creating the backup, such as which external hard drive to use, will be saved for all subsequent backups. This is useful if you want to run the backup on a regular schedule. If you want to create a different backup, you will need to change the settings by clicking  Change settings in the *Backup and Restore* window.

**Tip**

**Check by Windows**

*Windows* itself will also check whether it is time to create a new full backup, and will display a message if too much time has elapsed since the last full backup.

 **Close all the windows** ¹

# 3.10 Restoring Personal Files

You can use the *Backup and Restore* window to restore a backup, if that is needed.

**Please note:**

Only perform the operations for restoring a backup, as described in this section, if you really want to restore a backup, for example, if you have lost data.

**☞ If necessary, connect the external hard drive to your computer**

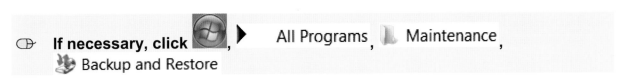

**If necessary, click** ▶ All Programs, Maintenance, Backup and Restore

You will see the *Backup and Restore* window:

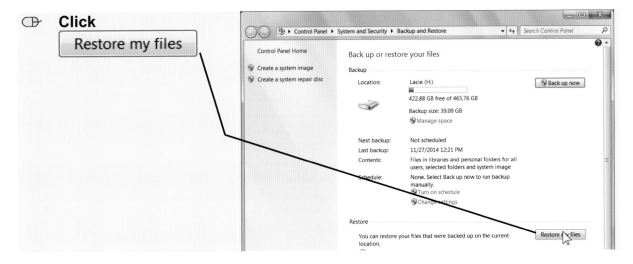

**Click** Restore my files

In the next window you can indicate which folders or files you want to restore. This is what you need to do in order to restore one or more folders:

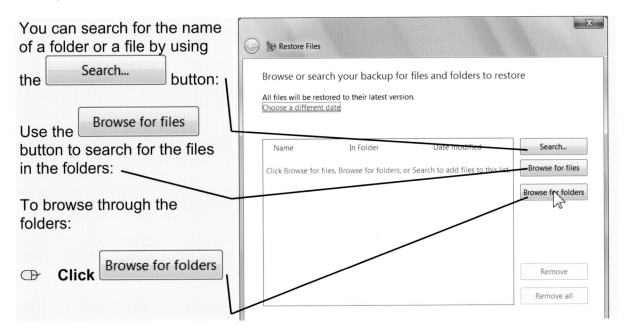

You can search for the name of a folder or a file by using the Search... button:

Use the Browse for files button to search for the files in the folders:

To browse through the folders:

**Click** Browse for folders

Now you will see this window:

The backup folder contains all the folders and files from previous backups.

You can open a folder by double-clicking it:

☞ **Double-click the backup folder**

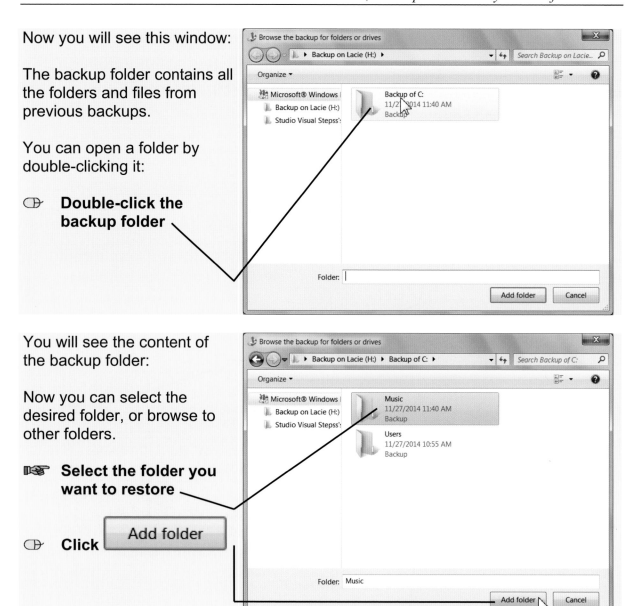

You will see the content of the backup folder:

Now you can select the desired folder, or browse to other folders.

☞ **Select the folder you want to restore**

☞ **Click** Add folder

## Tip

**Restore all the folders and files**
If you want to restore all the folders and files in a backup, you need to click the

 Backup of C:
11/27/2014 11:40 AM
Backup                  folder, which contains the full backup, and then click

 . But keep in mind that only the data files will be restored; any programs or *Windows* components will not be restored.

The folder has been added to the list and will be restored: ⎯

☞ **Repeat these steps for each folder you want to restore**

You can use the

Remove

and

Remove all

buttons to delete folders and files from the list: ⎯

☞ **Click** Next

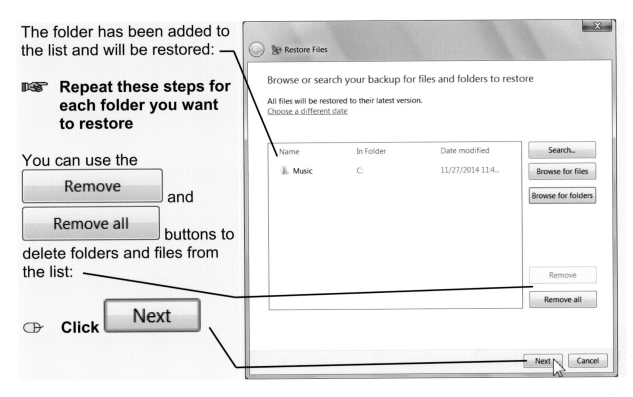

In most cases, the files you restore will replace the original files on your computer. But you can also restore the files to a different location if your original hard drive has been damaged.

In this example we have chosen to restore the files to their original location:

You can select a different location by clicking the radio button ◉ by
**In the following location:** ,
and browsing to the desired folder: ⎯

☞ **Click** Restore

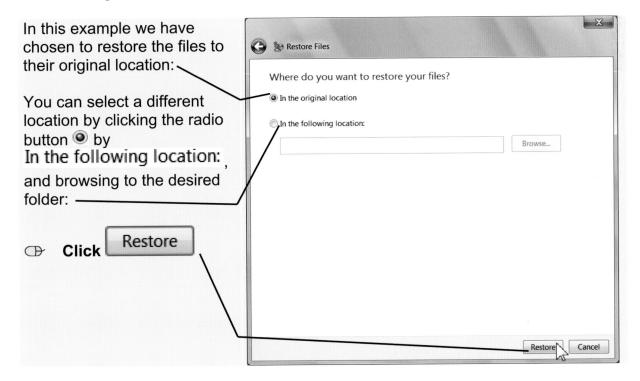

If your computer's hard drive contains any folders and files that have the same name, and are stored in the same location, you will see the window below. You can decide which action to take for each individual file:

Replace the file on the hard drive by the file you are restoring:

Do not restore the file:

Restore the file, but give it a different name:

To use the same option for all the files that are going to be restored:

☞ **Check the box ☑ by Do this for all conflic**

☞ **Click the desired option**

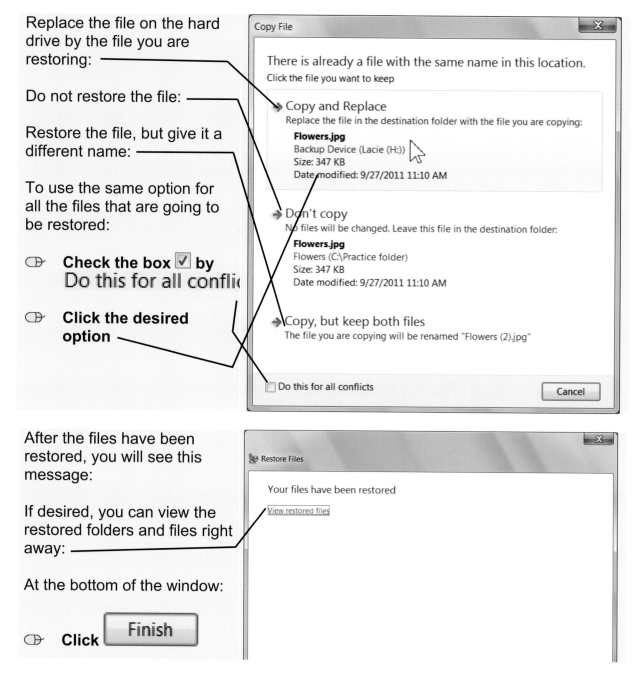

After the files have been restored, you will see this message:

If desired, you can view the restored folders and files right away:

At the bottom of the window:

☞ **Click** [ Finish ]

You have just restored (part of) a backup.

 **Close all the windows** ✆¹

# 3.11 Creating a System Image

In *Windows 7* you can create a full backup. This type of backup is also called a *system image* or *system copy*. A system image contains copies of your programs, system settings, and files. You can use a system image to restore the content of your computer if your hard drive crashes or the computer stops working for other reasons.

☞ **If necessary, connect the external hard drive to your computer**

☞ **Click** , ▶ All Programs , Maintenance , Backup and Restore

You will see the *Backup and Restore* window:

☞ **Click**
Create a system image

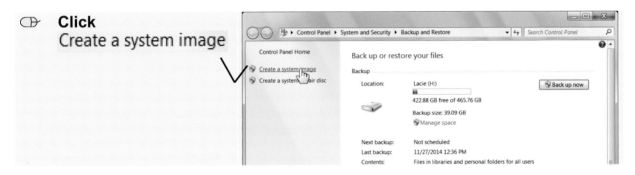

The next steps for creating a system image are the same as with *Windows 8.1*. You can follow the steps starting at *section 3.4 Creating a System Image*.

☞ **Continue on page 132**

# 3.12 Copying Personal Files to an External Hard Drive

You do not need to do a full backup, if you just want to make a copy of a few files for safekeeping. If the files are small, or if you want to be able to use them on other computers, you can copy them to an external hard drive in the usual way. In *Windows 7* you can do this using the *Computer* window.

In *section 3.5 Copying Personal Files to an External Hard Drive*, you can read how to copy these files. The copying method is the same for both *Windows 7* and *Windows 8.1*:

☞ **Continue on page 137**

# 3.13 Creating Restore Points

There is always a chance that *Windows 7* suddenly stops working. This may happen for instance, after installing a new program. If the problem solving tools have not helped you, you can use the *System Restore* function.

With this program you can revert your computer to a *restore point*, that is to say, to a previous state of the computer. You can select a date when you know that *Windows* was working normally. This restore point is a reflection of the status of the stored system files on the computer at that time.

 **Please note:**

The *System Restore* program will only save changes in the operating system and in certain application files. If you restore the system to a previous state by using a restore point, this will not affect your personal data files. Your text files, email messages, photos, etc. will not be changed.

This means you cannot use *System Restore* to undo the deletion of a document, email or photo.

*Windows 7* automatically creates restore points on a daily basis, and also when major changes are made, such as the installation of new programs or devices. If necessary, you can create a restore point manually before making major changes. You can do that as follows:

☞ **Open the *Control Panel*** $\mathscr{O}\mathscr{O}^3$

⊕ **Click** System and Security, System, 🛡 System protection

The next steps are the same as those described earlier in *section 3.6 Creating Restore Points*. You can continue from there.

☞ **Continue on page 139**

# 3.14 Reverting to Restore Points

If you experience any problem with your system after an update or after you have installed a device, you can revert the system to a restore point as described in this section.

 **Please note:**

If you have used the *System Restore* program, your computer will need to be restarted. This means you need to close all your programs and save your work before using the *System Restore* program.

The *System Restore* program in *Windows 7* works the same way as in *Windows 8.1*. You can follow the steps starting at *section 3.7 Reverting to a Restore Point*:

☞ **Continue on page 141**

**HELP! I cannot find the program.**

You can find the *System Restore* program in the *Accessories* folder:

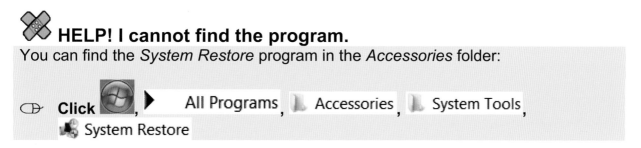

In this chapter you have learned how to create backups, restore points and how to revert back to a restore point. You have also learned how to create a system image.

# 3.15 Background Information

**Dictionary**

| | |
|---|---|
| **Backup** | A backup is an extra copy, or safety copy of the data stored on a computer. A copy is made as a preventive measure to secure important data, in case the data on the original storage medium is lost or damaged. A backup can be restored, if necessary. |
| **File history** | A backup that includes previous versions of personal files. |
| **Incremental backup** | In this type of backup only the new and changed files are saved, and not the files included in a previous backup. |
| **Personal files** | Files that you have personally saved on your computer. For example, photos, videos, music, documents, spreadsheets, etc. |
| **Restore point** | The representation of a stored status of the system files on the computer. You can use restore points to restore the system files on your computer and revert to a previous state. |
| **System image** | A system image is an exact copy of a hard drive. It is essentially a full backup. A system image by default, will contain the disk drives that are essential for running *Windows*. The system image contains the *Windows* operating system and your system settings, programs and files. You can use a system image to restore the content of your computer if the hard drive crashes or the computer for some other reason has stopped working. If you decide to restore a system image to your computer, it is an all-embracing process. You cannot restore individual items. All your current programs, system settings and files will be replaced by the content of the system image. |

*Source: Windows Help and Support, Wikipedia*

## External hard drives

You can buy two types of external hard drives. The first type is an external hard drive that is able to function all by itself. It is connected to the USB or firewire port of the computer by a cable. Some brands have an on/off switch while others are turned on only when you connect them to the computer.

The second type of external hard drive is one that is inserted into a special slot in the computer casing. This slot is wide opening where you can fit the hard drive, usually with a flap to prevent dust from coming in. Since each hard drive has its own unique shape and connecting points, the device needs to match the brand and type of slot that is used. This is why you cannot insert a regular external hard drive into such a slot.

Sometimes, this type of external hard drive can be used outside of the computer by connecting it with a cable. This is useful if you want to use the device with another computer that is not equipped with a special slot.

External hard drives are slower than internal hard drives. You can get external hard drives for a USB 2.0 connection or for the faster 3.0 connection.

External hard drives are available in different speeds. Currently, 5400 and 7200 revolutions per minute are the norm. You can buy even faster drives, but they are more expensive. The SSD are the fastest, since they do not have any moveable parts.

The current capacity of external hard drives ranges from 100 Gigabyte (GB) up to as high 8 terabytes as of this writing. 1000 Gigabytes is 1 Terabyte (TB).

Because of their extremely large capacity, external hard drives are very suitable for storing a great quantity of files or for very large files, such as videos in HD format. Make sure to buy an external hard drive with as much capacity as you can afford. The drive will fill up quicker than you think.

# 3.16 Tips

 **Tip**

## Export favorite bookmarks

The *Internet Explorer* browser saves the addresses of your favorite websites as favorites (bookmarks). You can store these on an external hard drive. In this way, you will always have a backup copy of your bookmarks. You can save them by exporting them. You can do this in *Internet Explorer* as follows:

☞ **Open *Internet Explorer* ⅍⁴**

⊕ **Click ⭐**

⊕ **By** Add to favorites

**click ▾**

⊕ **Click** ⁞⮑ Import and export...

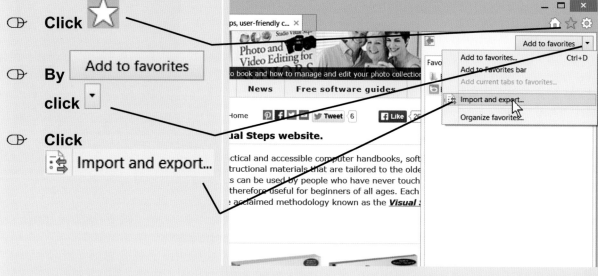

You will see the *Import/Export Settings* window:

⊕ **Click the radio button**
   ◉ **by** Export to a file

⊕ **Click** Next >

*- Continue on the next page -*

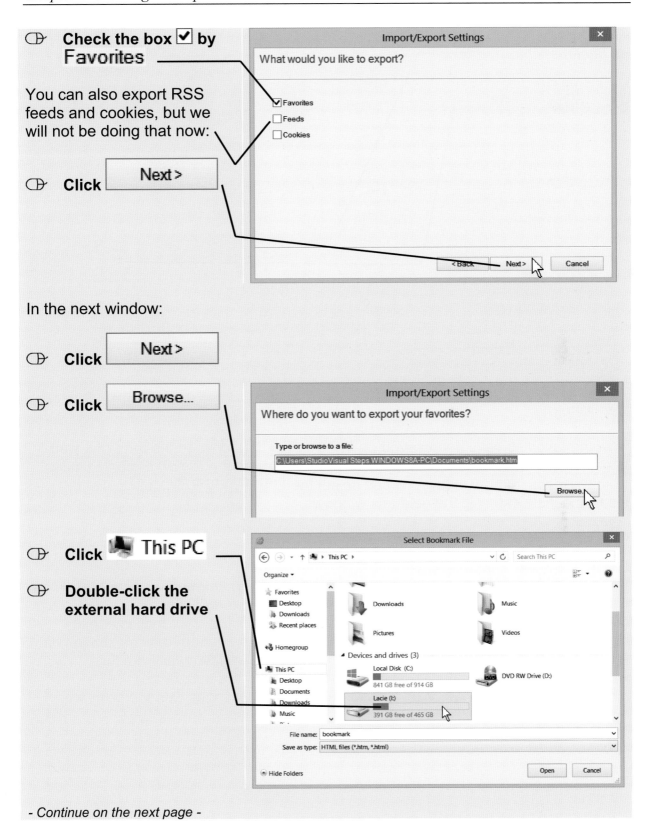

- Continue on the next page -

The favorites will be stored as *bookmark.htm*:

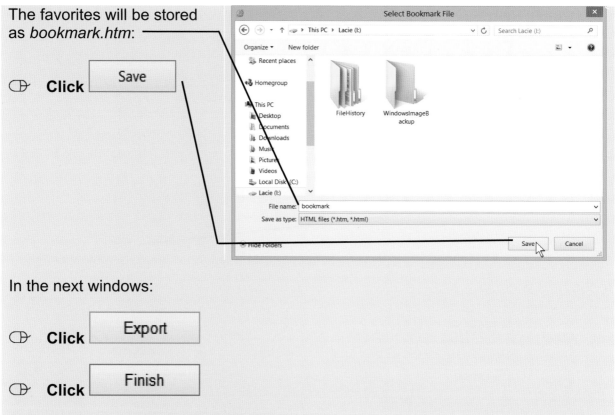

☞ **Click** Save

In the next windows:

☞ **Click** Export

☞ **Click** Finish

Now the favorites have been saved on the external hard drive in the form of a web page. In order to restore the favorites, you need to open the *Import/Export Settings* window again. In this window you can select the Import from a file option. Then follow the instructions in the next few windows.

 **Tip**
**Export Email in Windows Live Mail**
You can also save the email you have sent and received in *Windows Live Mail* on an external hard drive. This is not possible if you are using the *Mail* app or *Outlook.com* on a *Windows 8.1* computer. But, this is not a problem since your mail is already stored online by the mail servers. If you still want to export your email messages on a *Windows 8.1* computer, it is best to download *Windows Live Mail* from the webpage http://windows.microsoft.com/en-us/windows-live/essentials-other#essentials=overviewother, retrieve your email messages with the program, and then perform the following steps.

*- Continue on the next page -*

This is how you export mail in *Windows Live Mail*:

☞ **Open *Windows Live Mail* ✂8**

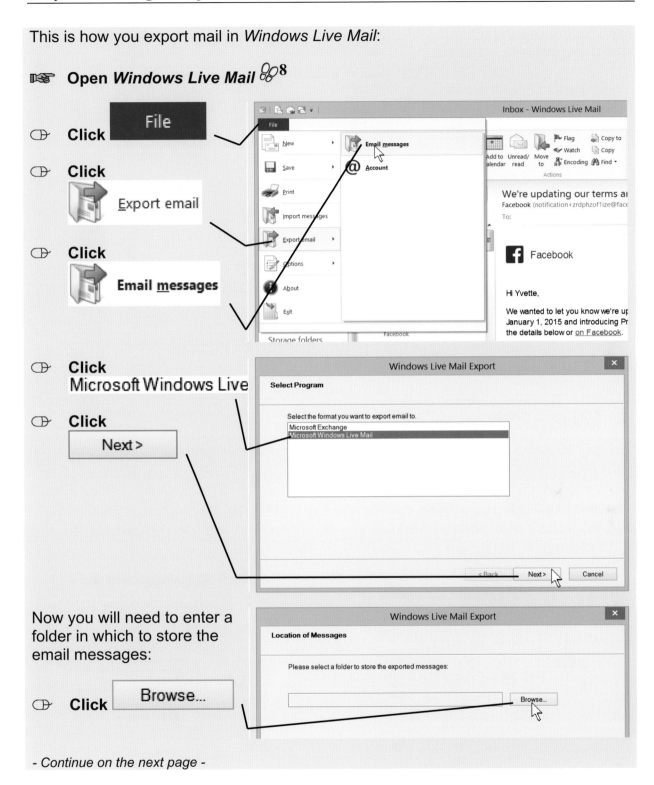

**Click** File

**Click** Export email

**Click** Email messages

**Click** Microsoft Windows Live

**Click** Next >

Now you will need to enter a folder in which to store the email messages:

**Click** Browse...

*- Continue on the next page -*

☞ **Select the external hard drive**

If you want to create a new folder, click

| Make New Folder |:

⊕ **Click** | OK |

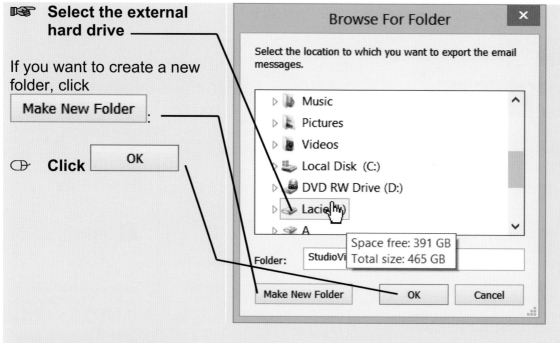

In the next few windows:

⊕ **Click** | Next > | twice

⊕ **Click** | Finish |

Now the email has been saved to your external hard drive. If something goes wrong with the folders in *Windows Live Mail*, you can import the exported email messages into the program again:

⊕ **Click** | File |

⊕ **Click**

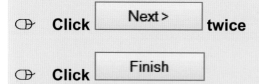

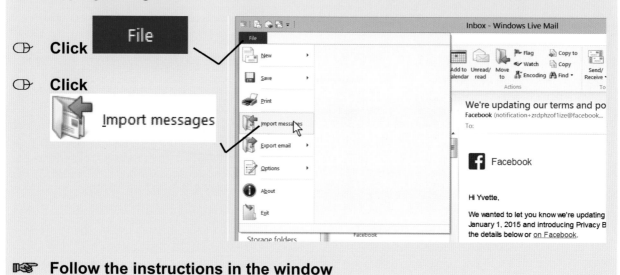

☞ **Follow the instructions in the window**

**Tip**

**Cloud backup**

More and more companies, such as *Microsoft*, *Google*, and others, are creating online storage services that allow you to store a backup online. This means you use the Internet to place a backup on the company's servers. This is called an online backup, or a *cloud* backup.

The fees charged for these services often depend on the amount of data you store. Usually, there is a certain amount of free storage, often a few GBs. An important advantage is the fact that the backup is safely stored outside your house. In the case of fire or other natural disaster, you will always have access to your files when you are ready. The provider also makes sure the data they store is securely backed up.

If you want to create a cloud backup, it is important that you have a fast Internet connection. This goes for the upload speed (to the cloud) as well as for the download speed (to your computer).

 **Tip**

**View the file history in the Windows 8.1 PC Settings**

In this chapter you have seen how you can use the *Control Panel* to set up the file history and create backups. You can also do this with the *PC Settings* charm in *Windows 8.1*:

☞ **Open the *PC Settings* app** 16

On the left-hand side of the screen:

⬡ Click **Update and recovery**

⬡ Click **File History**

You will see that the file history has been turned on, and the name of the device used for the backup:

To create a backup, click

**Back up now**.

# Notes

Write your notes down here.

# 4. Cleaning Up Your Computer

A lot of data is temporarily stored or cached on your computer. Every now and then, it is a good idea to remove this unnecessary data.

You can use *Disk Cleanup* to delete superfluous files from your hard drive. *Optimize Drives* (in *Windows 8.1*) or *Disk Defragmenter* (in *Windows 7*) enhance the performance of your computer by collecting files and remnants of files that have spread out all over your computer. These tools will remove superfluous files and re-arrange others in an optimal order so that *Windows* can find them more quickly. The computer will then work more efficiently.

The speed of your computer is determined by its components. Programs always require a certain minimum level of performance from these components in order to work properly. In *Windows* you can view the components that make up your computer and see how they perform. If desired, you can use this information to upgrade your computer by purchasing better components.

Besides the tools that come with *Windows*, you can also use other utility software to clean up your computer. For instance, the free *CCleaner* program will help you quickly and safely clean up your computer.

When you turn on your computer, a number of programs will start up automatically along with *Windows*. Some of these programs are important, such as an antivirus program. But sometimes they are less essential. By managing these startup programs with *CCleaner*, you can make your computer startup a little faster and work more efficiently.

In this chapter you will learn how to:

- clean up the hard drive;
- uninstall programs;
- work with *Check Disk*;
- defrag or optimize a drive;
- view and use system info;
- clean up with *CCleaner*;
- manage startup programs with *CCleaner*.

# 4.1 Cleaning Up Your Hard Drive

As you use your computer, your hard drive slowly collects temporary files. For a large part, this happens automatically, for example, while you are surfing the Internet. After a while it is a good idea to do a thorough spring-cleaning and remove these temporary files. If your computer becomes too full, this is really essential. You can view the amount of space you have left in *Windows Explorer* by clicking *This PC* (in *Windows 8.1*) or *Computer* (in *Windows 7*):

☞ **Open the *This PC* or the *Computer* window in *Windows Explorer* ☙⁹⁰10**

Some of the *Explorer* views do not display the available disk space on the hard drive(s). If you do not see the available disk space, you need to change the view.

In *Windows 8.1*:

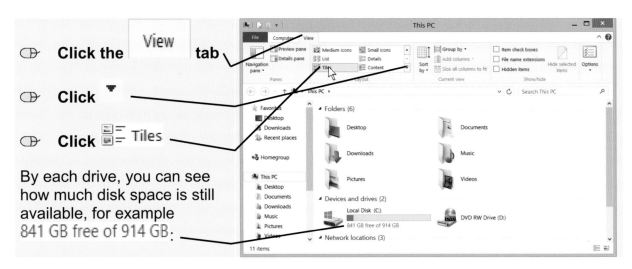

In *Windows 7*:

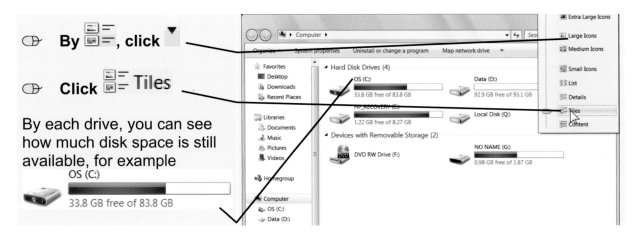

**Tip**

**10% free space**
The rule of thumb is to have at least 10% of free disk space available of the total storage capacity, but preferably more. From experience, we know that a computer slows down when the hard drive fills up, and this can lead to all sorts of problems. This is often caused by the multitude of programs that use the hard drive as a temporary storage space for data. If there is not enough free space, these programs start to 'choke', as it were, and will cause hiccups. If there is too little free space on the C drive, a warning message will appear in the taskbar.

There is a tool you can use to clean up the hard drive. This is how you open it:

☞ **Click the hard drive, for example**

Local Disk (C:)

841 GB free of 914 GB

☞ **Right-click the hard disk**

☞ **Click** Properties

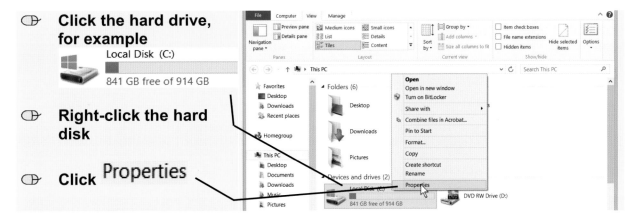

The *Properties of Local Disk (C:)* or *Local Disk (C:)* window will be opened. The drive may have a different name on your own computer.

In this screenshot you can see the distribution of used and free space:

☞ **Click** Disk Cleanup

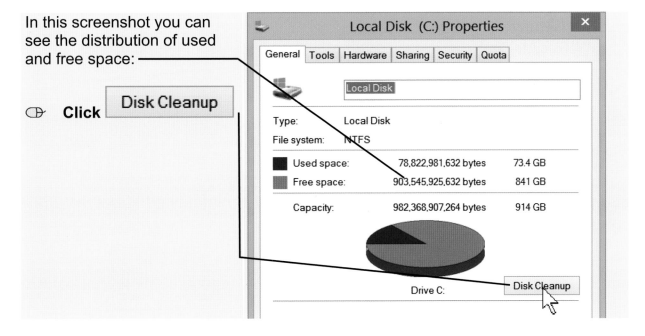

You will see the *Disk Cleanup* tool:

If your computer has multiple hard drives, you will see this window:

☞ **Select the hard drive you want to clean up**

⊕ **Click** ⌷ OK ⌷

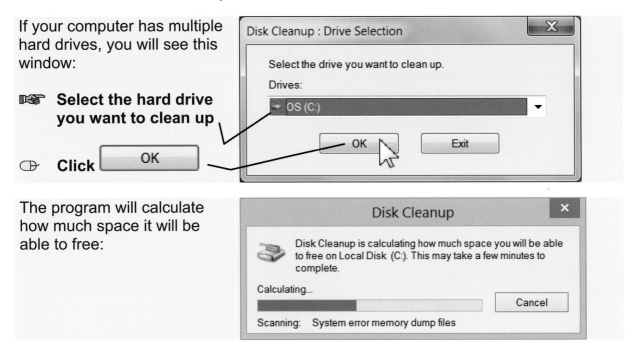

The program will calculate how much space it will be able to free:

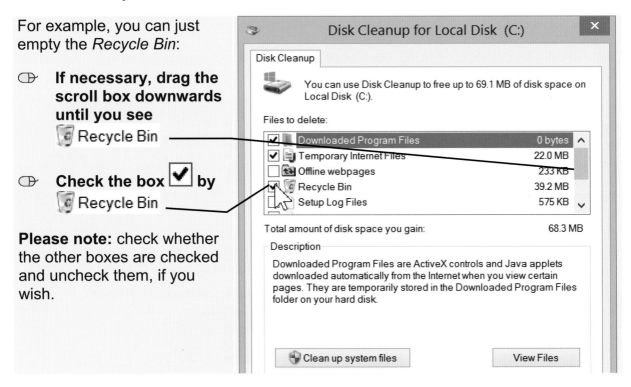

In this window you can choose which files to delete:

For example, you can just empty the *Recycle Bin*:

⊕ **If necessary, drag the scroll box downwards until you see** 🗑 Recycle Bin

⊕ **Check the box ☑ by** 🗑 Recycle Bin

**Please note:** check whether the other boxes are checked and uncheck them, if you wish.

Here you can view each selected item (in blue) and see what will be deleted:

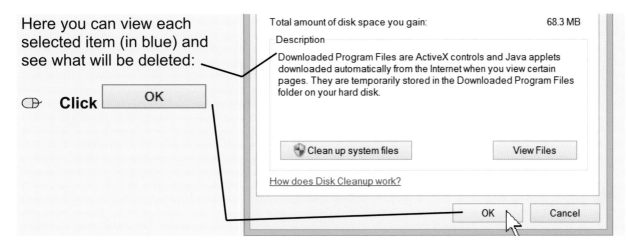

 **Click** OK

---

## Tip

**Default settings for Disk Cleanup**

If you are using the *Disk Cleanup* tool, you can usually delete all the checked items without experiencing any problems.

You will be asked to confirm this action:

 **Click** Delete Files

The tool cleans the drive and removes the unnecessary files:

 **Close all the windows** **1**

## Tip

**Unnecessary programs**

Is your computer becoming too full? In that case, you can always consider deleting the programs you hardly ever use. In the next section you can read how to do that.

# 4.2 Uninstalling Programs

Your computer may contain some programs you seldom use or never use at all. You can easily remove these programs.

When you install a program onto your computer, you actually install both the program and an additional uninstall program at the same time. The uninstall program cleans up all the program files and will remove the program buttons or icons from the Start screen, the Start menu and even the Desktop. This is called uninstalling.

 **Please note:**

Do not use *Windows Explorer* to remove programs. If you use this method, remnants of the program can remain stored on the computer which eventually makes the computer run slower.

In this example we will remove the *Adobe Reader* program. Other programs can be uninstalled the same way.

☞ **Open the *Control Panel*** 👣3

☞ **By Programs, click Uninstall a program**

You will see the list of programs that can be uninstalled. In this example we have selected 📕 Adobe Reader XI.

 **Please note:**

The list of programs often contains programs that are essential for your computer to function properly. Do you see an unfamiliar program? Do not uninstall it. First try to find out what the program's function is. You can search the Internet or try using the Help function in *Windows*, for example.

First, you select the program:

☞ **Click**
    📕 Adobe Reader XI

Now you can delete the program:

☞ **Click Uninstall**

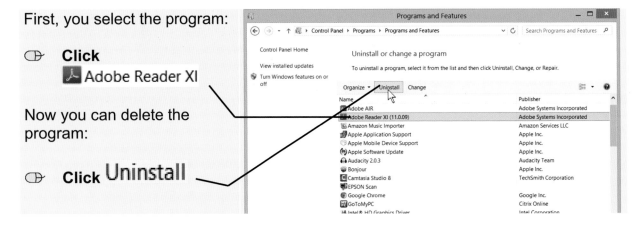

If you really want to delete the program:

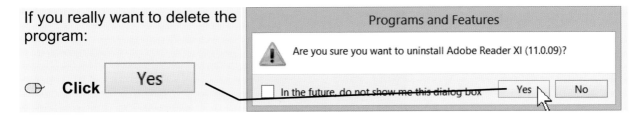

CB **Click** `Yes`

Your screen may turn dark. You will see a window where you need to give permission to continue.

☞ **If necessary, give permission to continue**

The program has been deleted:

☞ **Close the *Control Panel*** ¹

In *Windows 8.1*, apps are used along with the regular programs. If you no longer use an app, you can delete it:

☞ **Go to the Start screen** 👣²

CB **Place the pointer in the bottom left corner of the screen** ———

CB **Click**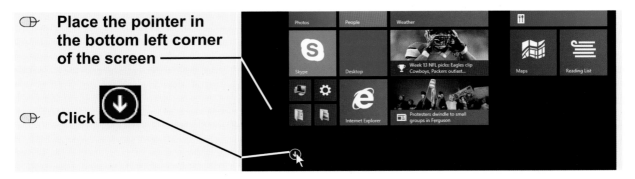

 **Please note:**
You can only delete the apps you have installed yourself. You cannot delete the apps that are included in the *Windows* operating system.

Right-click the app

Click Uninstall

You will see a warning message:

Click **Uninstall**

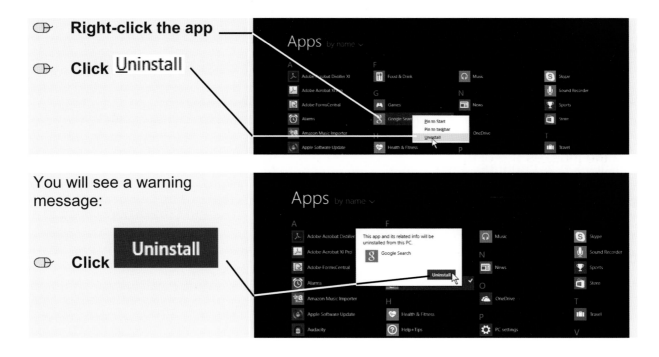

# 4.3 Check Disk

The hard drive is one of the few mechanically operated moving parts in the computer. Since mechanical parts can wear out, you need to check the hard drive at regular intervals. With the *Check Disk* utility, also called *Error Checking*, *Windows* checks the surface of the disk, and marks the sectors that may be damaged. These sectors will not be used any longer. If these sectors contain data, *Check Disk* will try to save it and move it to a safer spot. The operation will result in higher reliability and also in higher speed of the disk, because data that is stored in a damaged sector can only be retrieved after numerous attempts.

## Please note:

Some of the most modern computers are equipped with SSD (Solid State Drive). This is a different type of drive that is more similar to the memory chips in your computer than it is to traditional hard drives. An SSD does not have any moving parts, and that is why it is much faster. It is often used as a C: drive, alongside a regular hard drive. Because *Windows* and other important programs are usually installed on the C: drive, *Windows* will work much faster if it is installed on an SSD. You do not need to use the *Check Disk* program on an SSD, since these types of drives do not contain an actual disk like a regular hard drive.

You can check the manual that came with your computer, or the receipt, to find out whether your computer is equipped with an SSD.

It is best to use *Check Disk* before defragmenting or optimizing your computer (see *section 4.4 Optimizing or Defragmenting*). Then *Windows* will know which parts of the hard drive are untrustworthy while defragmenting, and will not store data there.

The *Check Disk* program checks to verify that:
- the files are stored in the proper place, that is, the place where they are supposed to be according to the content of the drive.
- the indexes are okay.
- the so-called 'security descriptions' are correct. These indicate who is the owner of a file, who has access to it, and what can be done with the file.
- the file data is correct and matches the contents of the files. This is compared to the checkpoint data within the file.
- untrustworthy areas are found on the remaining free space on the hard drive.

In *Windows*, you can use the *Explorer* window *This PC* (in *Windows 8.1*) or *Computer* (in *Windows 7*) to check a hard drive for errors:

☞ **Open the *This PC* window or the *Computer* window in *Explorer*** ✂10

⌦ **Click the desired hard drive**

⌦ **Right-click the hard drive**

⌦ **Click** Properties

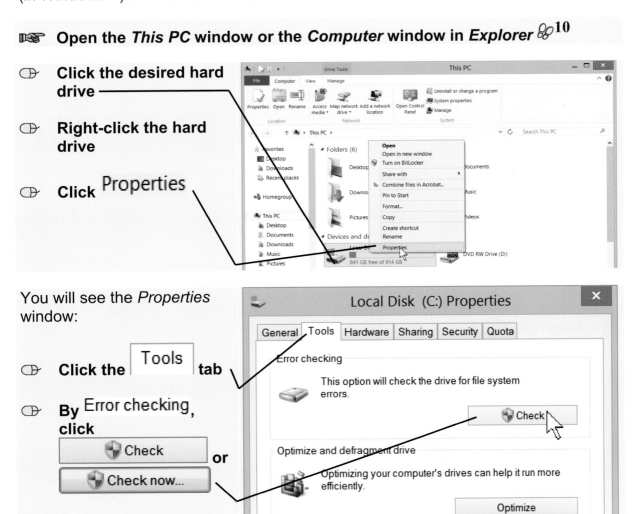

You will see the *Properties* window:

⌦ **Click the** Tools **tab**

⌦ **By** Error checking, **click** 🛡 Check **or** 🛡 Check now...

Your screen may now turn dark and you will see a window where you need to give permission to continue.

☞ **If necessary, give permission to continue**

*Windows 8.1* may already have checked the hard drive for errors and determined that there are none. In that case, you will see this window:

If you want to scan for errors anyway:

⊕ **Click ➡ Scan drive**

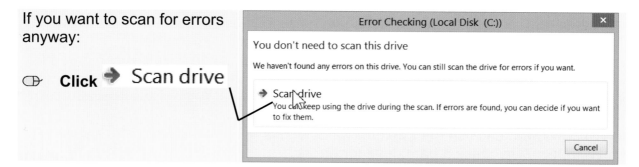

If you have decided to scan anyway, the scanning process may take a while. If any errors are found, you will see the error messages while the scan is performed. If there are no errors, you will see this window:

⊕ **Click** Close

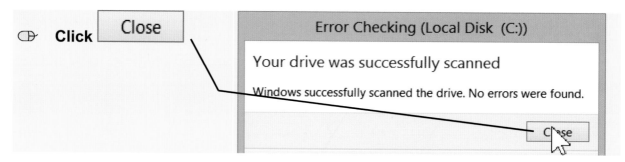

In *Windows 7*:

⊕ **Check the box ✔ by Automatically fix file sys**

⊕ **Check the box ✔ by Scan for and attempt**

⊕ **Click** Start

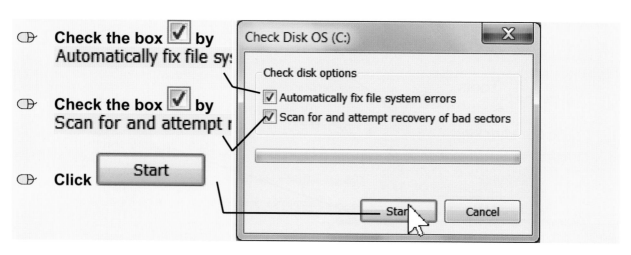

With the **Automatically fix file system errors** option, the system only checks to see if the data is stored in the correct spot on the drive. This can be done quite quickly. With the **Scan for and attempt recovery of bad sectors** option, the drive itself is checked for technical reliability. This can take much longer.

 **Please note:**

If the drive is large, *Check Disk* may take several hours, and will be performed when you restart the computer. If you want to postpone the check, you can click **Cancel** in the next window.

If the hard drive you want to check in *Windows 7* is in use, you will see this window:

In order to check the drive, next time the computer is started:

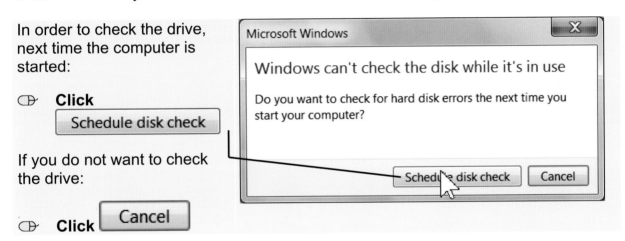

☞ **Click** **Schedule disk check**

If you do not want to check the drive:

☞ **Click** **Cancel**

 **Please note:**

Do you want to postpone the *Check Disk* utility from running, even after you have restarted the computer? Then you can press a key after the restart, as soon as you are asked to do so. If you do nothing after the restart, the *Check Disk* utility will start running. You will not be able to abort this operation.

If any errors have been found, you will see the error message during the process. Once the *Check Disk* process has finished, *Windows* will re-start.

 **HELP! Errors have been found on the drive.**

Normally you do not need to worry, if *Check Disk* finds errors on your hard drive. Over time, most hard drives will wear out, and the magnetic surface of the drive will have some small lesions and scratches.

*- Continue on the next page -*

By regularly checking your hard drive with *Check Disk*, the data in the damaged areas can often still be rescued. If you wait too long, the drive can develop more and more errors, become much slower, and the chances of losing information will increase.

Does the number of errors increase with every check? This may mean your hard drive needs to be replaced.

# 4.4 Optimizing or Defragmenting

In the course of time, your computer's hard drive will develop more errors, become more cluttered, and will contain more loose data fragments. Does it seem to take more time to open programs and save your work? If you have noticed this happening, you can try using the tools that will optimize or defrag your computer. All the files and fragments of files will be arranged in a neat order again. Your hard drive will be able to retrieve them quicker and easier.

Any untrustworthy sectors have already been marked by *Check Disk*, so they will not be used. If you have not already run *Check Disk*, you should do this first (see *section 4.3 Check Disk*).

 **Please note:**

*Optimizing* in *Windows 8.1* is the same thing as *Defragmenting* in *Windows 7*. In the remainder of this section we will use both terms.

 **Please note:**

Some of the newest computers are equipped with an SSD. In the previous section you have already read about these drives. You should not optimize or defrag an SSD. This can make the drive run slower.
You can check your computer manual or receipt to find out whether your computer uses an SSD.

 **Please note:**

In order to use *Disk Defragmenter*, you need at least 15% of free storage space on your hard drive. You cannot use *Disk Defragmenter* on an external hard drive.

This is how you start *Optimize*:

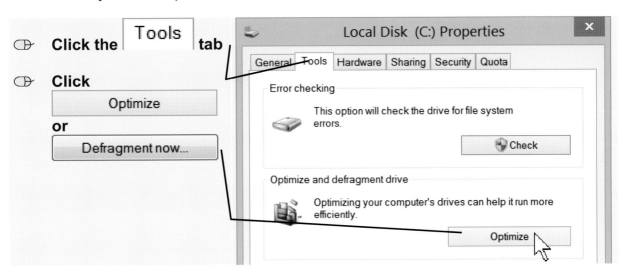

You will see the *Optimize Drives* window. The hard drive will be analyzed first:

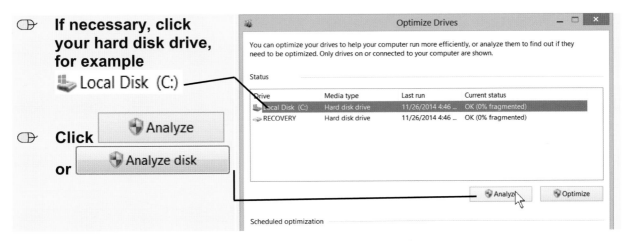

Your screen may turn dark, and you will see a window where you need to give permission to continue:

☞ **If necessary, give permission to continue**

If the drive will be defragmented for more than ten percent, it is recommended to optimize the drive.

Once the analysis has finished, you will see the percentage of defragmentation:

Usually, the optimizing operation is set to run on a weekly basis:

You can also start the optimization yourself:

👉 **Click** 🛡 Optimize

**or** 🛡 Defragment disk

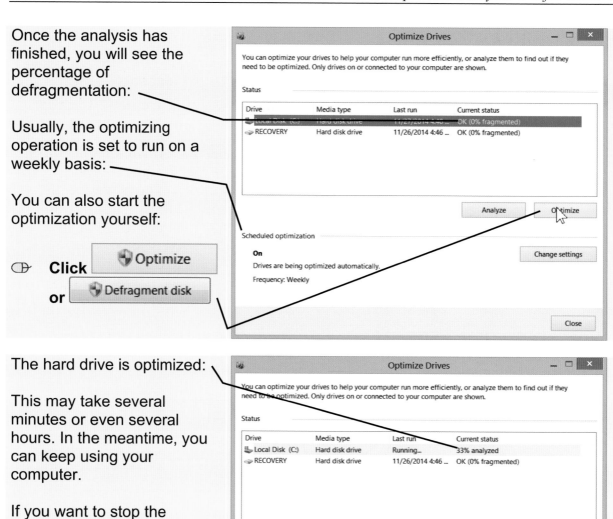

The hard drive is optimized:

This may take several minutes or even several hours. In the meantime, you can keep using your computer.

If you want to stop the optimization, click the

Stop **or**

🛡 Stop operation **buttons:**

When the optimization has finished, you can close the window:

At the bottom of the window:

👉 **Click** Close

👉 **Close all the windows** 👣1

# 4.5 Viewing System Info

Your computer's performance level is determined by a large number of factors. Important items in this are the *processor* and the *internal memory*, also called the *working memory* or *RAM* (*Random Access Memory*).

The performance of your computer can be important when you are going to buy new software, among other things. Each software program has its own requirements regarding the computer's components. If these components, and hence the performance of the computer, are not up to scratch, the software will not function properly. The minimum and optimum requirements for a computer are always specified on the software package, or on the manufacturer's website.

System information about your computer's components can also come in handy if a problem arises, and a helpdesk employee or repairman asks for this information.

Here is how to view the components in your computer:

☞ **Open the *Control Panel* ⁸⁸³**

⊕ **Click** System and Security , System

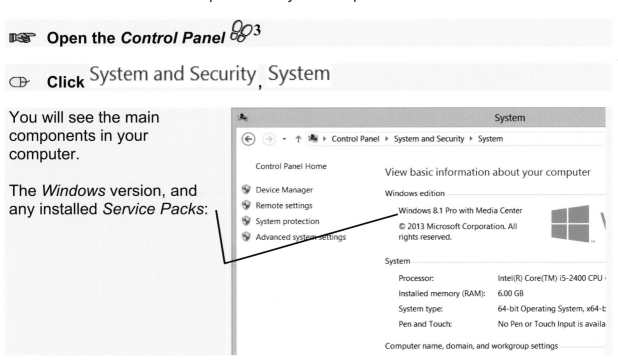

You will see the main components in your computer.

The *Windows* version, and any installed *Service Packs*:

After *Windows* was installed on your computer, there may have been recent adjustments and enhancements to the system in the form of *Windows updates*. These are installed automatically, if your computer is connected to the Internet and you have enabled the automatic update option. Major updates are called *Service Packs*. In *section 1.2 Updating Windows* you can read about checking for updates.

The brand and type of processor:

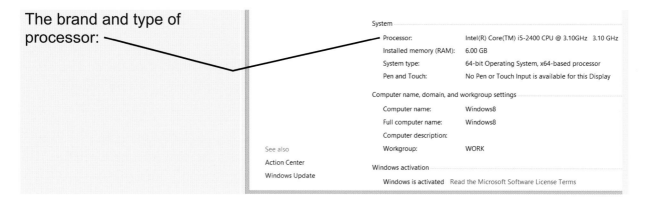

The processor is the core of your computer. All the operations you perform on your computer run through the processor. Modern processors compute at dazzling speed, with millions of operations per second. This speed is expressed in *megahertz* (MHz) or *gigahertz* (GHz). The higher the number, the faster the processor is, and the computer too.

The RAM memory:

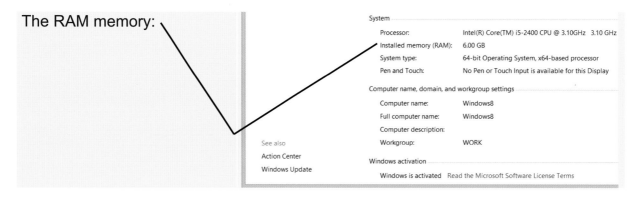

The RAM memory of the computer is the internal or working memory. *Windows*, the programs you use, and the work you are editing, are stored in the RAM memory while you work. This memory is much faster than the hard drive.

But you will need to save your work before you turn off or restart the computer, because the RAM memory can only remember data for the time the computer is turned on. The size of the RAM memory is expressed in *gigabytes* (GB).

 **Tip**

**Work faster with larger RAM memory**
If the RAM memory is larger, the data that is in use will not need to be opened from the slower hard drive, but can often be stored in the RAM memory. This will speed up your computer while you are working. Extending the RAM memory is a relatively cheap and simple way of speeding up your computer.

In *Windows* you will see the type of operating system by System type: ; this can be a 32 or 64-bit operating system: ————

A 64-bit version is faster than a 32-bit system. You can only use the 64-bit version of *Windows* if you have a processor that can handle that 64-bit version.

Here is the name of your computer:————

If you are using a network or homegroup, you will see the name by which your computer is known to others in this network or homegroup, by Computer description: .

You can see if your version of *Windows* has been activated by *Microsoft*:————

A non-active version can only be used for a limited period.

Here is the product code:

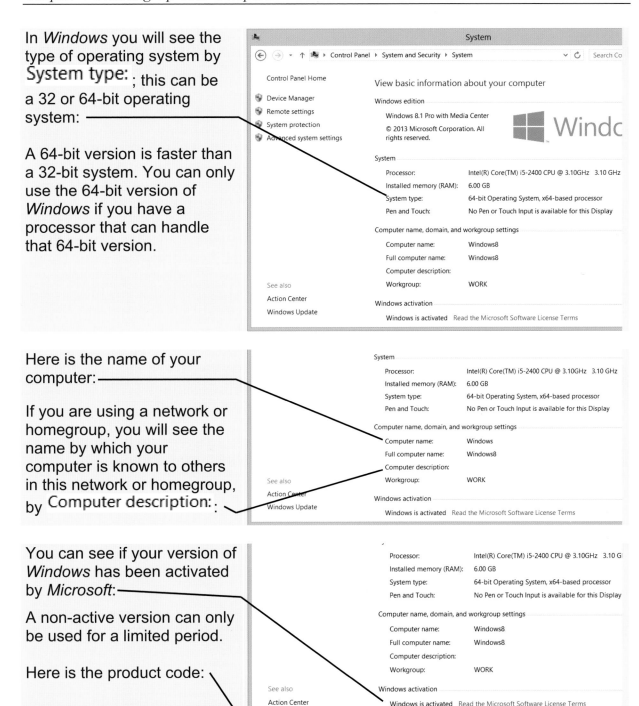

 **Please note:**

Never change the product code yourself! A different product code will need to be activated all over again and if you do not have the correct activation code, *Windows* will stop working.

☞ **Close the *System* window** 𝒢𝒢¹

# 4.6 Cleaning Up with CCleaner

If you want to clean up and manage your computer, you can make good use of the various *Windows* utilities. But there are also lots of programs on the market that are especially made for cleaning up your computer. They often provide various functions in a single, useful package. The free *CCleaner* program is such a program.

*CCleaner* has many options. One of these is cleaning up your computer. During the cleaning, all unnecessary files will be deleted, such as the temporary files used by *Windows*. The *Recycle Bin* will be emptied as well, among other things. This will free up space on your hard drive.

To safeguard your privacy, *CCleaner* can also delete any traces of your computer usage. For example, you can delete the history of the websites you have visited for each browser application installed on your computer. You can also delete the names of the files you have previously opened on your computer. This means that no one will be able to tell which files you have opened in a certain program.

*CCleaner* also lets you disable startup programs, in order to speed up the startup time of your computer. You can read more about this in the next section.

This is how you download and install the *CCleaner* program:

☞ **Open the www.piriform.com/ccleaner website** 𝒢𝒢¹¹

You will see the website of the *CCleaner* manufacturer:

☞ **Click**

**Free Download**

You can choose which version of *CCleaner* to install:

The paid versions have more options, but the free version will provide you with a good start:

By

click

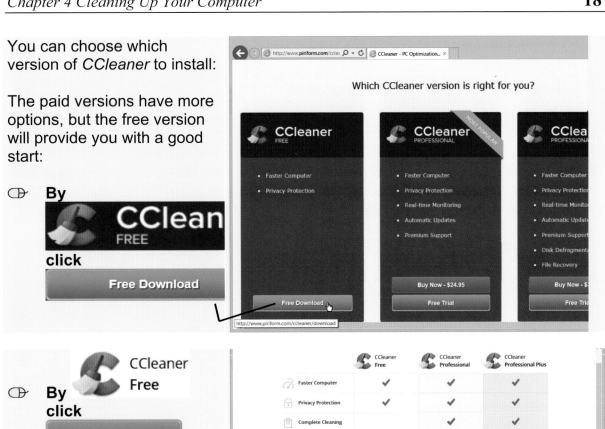

By

click

In *Internet Explorer*:

Click

If you are using *Mozilla Firefox*, click **Save File**, and in *Google Chrome* the file will be saved automatically.

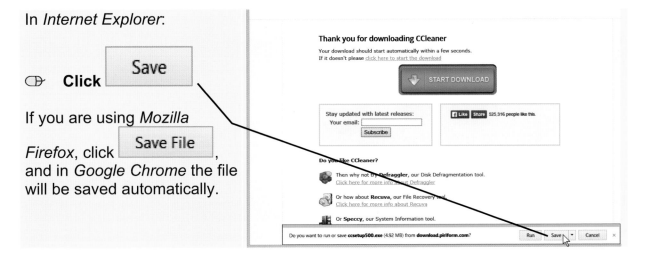

Once the file has been downloaded:

☞ **Close the Internet browser window** 🦶¹

Now you can install *CCleaner*:

☞ **Open *Windows Explorer*** 🦶14

Click 📁 Downloads

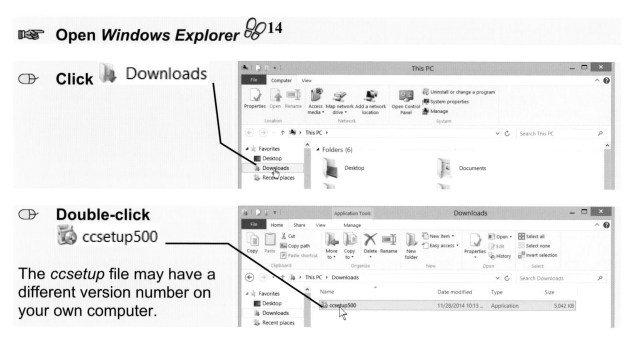

**Double-click**
🗑 ccsetup500

The *ccsetup* file may have a
different version number on
your own computer.

Your screen may now turn dark, and you will need to give permission to continue:

☞ **If necessary, give permission to continue**

The language is set to
English:

If this is not the case you can
change it by
Select your language:.

Click  Next >

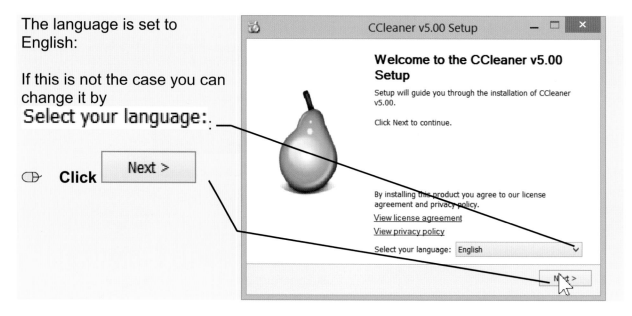

You can leave the settings as they are:

👉 **Click** Next >

If you already see the Install button:

👉 **Click** Install

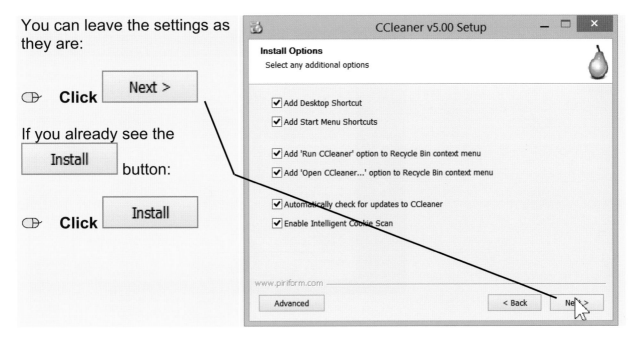

You may see this window first:

You do not need to install the *Google Toolbar*:

👉 **Uncheck the box** ☑ **by Install the free Goog**

At the bottom of the window:

👉 **Click** Install

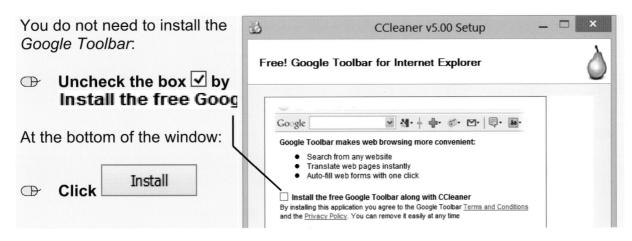

*CCleaner* will be installed. When this is done, you can open the program directly:

👉 **Uncheck the box** ☑ **by View Release notes**

At the bottom of the window:

👉 **Click** Finish

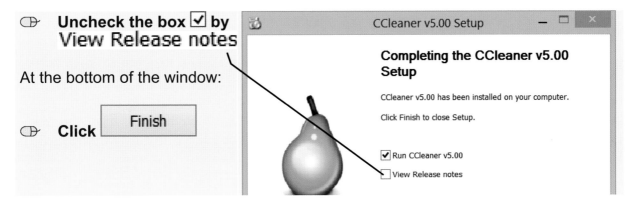

You will see the *CCleaner* window:

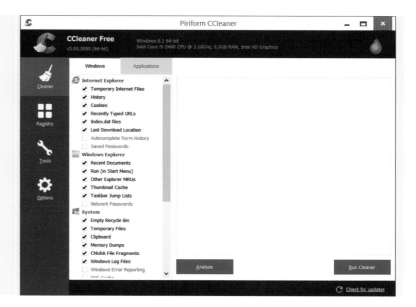

  **Tip**

**Opening CCleaner**

You can also open *CCleaner* from the Start screen, the Start menu, the list of all apps screen, or from a shortcut on your desktop.

To safely remove the unnecessary files from your computer, and clean up its main components to safeguard your privacy, you can simply use the default settings of the *CCleaner* program.

  **Please note:**

*CCleaner* will also delete the content of your *Recycle Bin*. If you do not want the files in your *Recycle Bin* to be deleted from your computer, you can change the settings in *CCleaner* and exclude this folder. You can also check the *Recycle Bin* first, and see if the files can be deleted. Just double-click the *Recycle Bin* icon on your desktop.
You should take into account that you will free up less space if you decide not to empty the *Recycle Bin*.

  **Please note:**

It is wise not to use the computer during the cleanup operation. This is because *CCleaner* also cleans up various components in your programs, such as Internet browser applications. It will not really do any damage if you keep using this program, but *CCleaner* will need to wait and see if it needs to change anything in a program you are using. You will see a message asking you to close the program before *CCleaner* can continue doing its job.

This is how you clean up your computer with *CCleaner*:

If you do not want to empty
the *Recycle Bin*:

☞ **Drag the scroll box**
**downwards**

☞ **Uncheck the box ☑ by**
Empty Recycle Bin

To clean up:

☞ **Click**
Run Cleaner

☞ **Click** OK

The process is started:

When *CCleaner* has finished, you will see a window showing details of the cleaning:

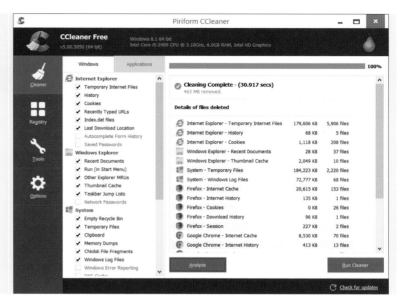

## 4.7 Managing Startup Programs with CCleaner

When you turn on your computer not only does the *Windows* operating system start up, but many other so-called startup programs will start up as well. These startup programs can of course slow down the startup process. They can also slow down the functioning of the computer in general, because they work in the background and take up memory space. For some programs, such as antivirus programs, it is essential that they start up right away. But for other programs you can disable them from starting up automatically to help your computer start faster and run more efficiently.

In *Windows* you can view the list of programs that startup automatically and remove some of them, if desired. *Microsoft* offers a good tool for this function, called *Autoruns* that can be downloaded separately. But this program is quite technical and meant for more advanced users.
Because of this, we will be using the *CCleaner* program in this book. This program lets you view and disable startup programs as well, but in a much easier way. All the add-ons or plugins that start up for your Internet browser applications will also be displayed. Plugins (or add-ons) are additions to the application which can slow down the functioning of the browser.

This is how you can view the list of programs that start up automatically:

☞ **Open** *CCleaner* 🦶🦶 12

Click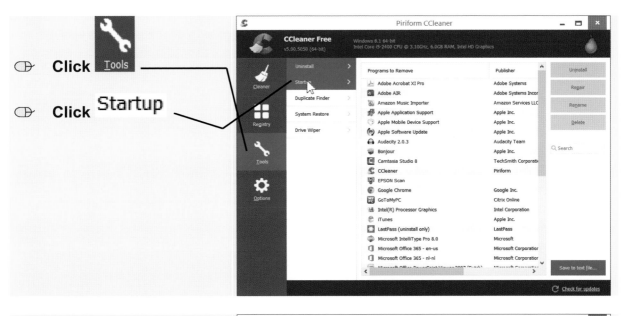

Click Tools

Click **Startup**

All the startup programs will be displayed: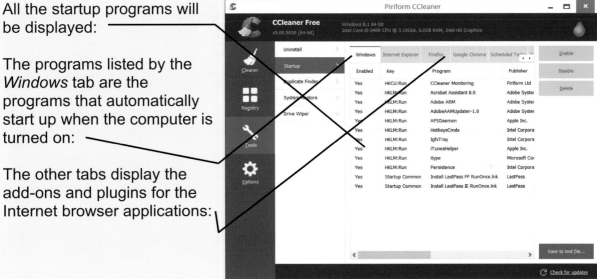

The programs listed by the *Windows* tab are the programs that automatically start up when the computer is turned on:

The other tabs display the add-ons and plugins for the Internet browser applications:

You can prevent a program from automatically starting up by disabling it. This will not delete the program from the startup folders, but will make sure the program does not start up when *Windows* is started.

 **Please note:**

Disabling antivirus programs, drivers and communication programs in the startup folders may cause your computer to dysfunction. You should only disable a program in the list if you are sure what its function is. If a problem does arise, you can always re-enable the program later.

In order to disable a program at startup:

☞ **Click the desired program**

☞ **Click**

Disable

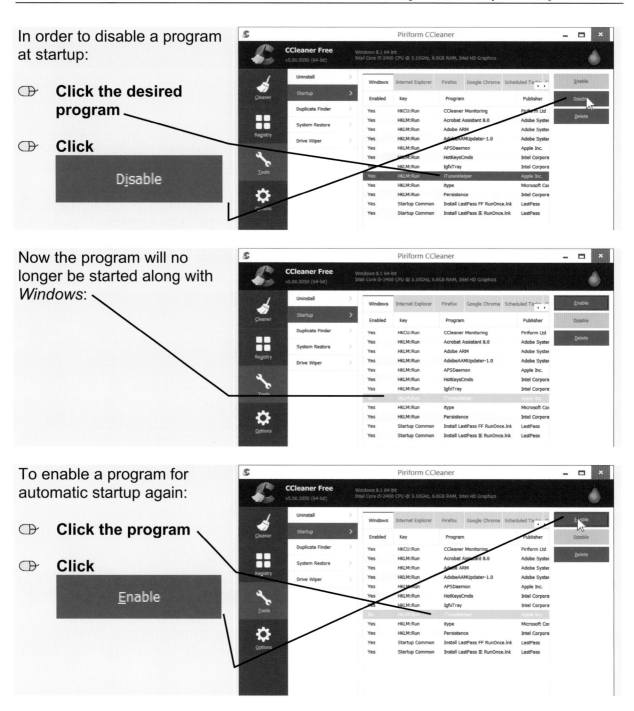

Now the program will no longer be started along with *Windows*:

To enable a program for automatic startup again:

☞ **Click the program**

☞ **Click**

Enable

☞ **Close the window** 👣¹

In this chapter you have learned how to clean up the hard drive, uninstall programs, and work with *Check Disk*. You have also learned how to optimize the computer and view the system info. Besides all this, you have learned how to use some of the options in the *CCleaner* program.

# 4.8 Visual Steps Website

By now we hope you have noticed that the Visual Steps method is an excellent method for quickly and efficiently learning more about tablets, computers, other devices and software applications. All books published by Visual Steps use this same method. In various series, we have published a large number of books on a wide variety of topics including *Windows*, *Mac OS X*, the iPad, iPhone, Samsung Galaxy Tab, Kindle, photo editing and many other interesting subjects.

**Website**
On the **www.visualsteps.com** website you will find a full product summary by clicking the blue *Catalog* button. Each book has a website accompanying it where you will find an extensive description of the book, the full table of contents, and a sample chapter (as a PDF file). You can use this information to find out if the title meets your expectations. You can also order the book directly online from this website.

On this informative website you will also find these items, among other things:
- free computer booklets and information guides (PDF files) on various subjects;
- separate web pages containing information about photo and video editing;
- frequently asked questions and their answers;
- information about the free Computer Certificate you can acquire on the online test website **www.ccforseniors.com**;
- free email notification service: receive an email when a certain book is published.

# 4.9 Background Information

**Dictionary**

| | |
|---|---|
| **Autoruns** | A tool or utility that provides detailed information about the programs that start up automatically when you start *Windows*. This program can be downloaded for free from Microsoft. |
| **CCleaner** | A utility program that can be used to clean up your computer, delete traces of Internet and file usage, and manage startup programs. |
| **Check Disk** | *Check Disk*, also called *Disk Error*, in *Windows* checks the surface of the drive and marks areas that may be damaged. These areas will no longer be used. If these areas contain data, the *Check Disk* function will try to save it and move it to a secure spot. Apart from a higher level of reliability, this will also result in higher speed, because the data that is stored in a damaged area is more difficult to retrieve; often it takes several attempts to retrieve this data. |
| **Defragmentation** | A term used in *Windows 7* for *Optimize,* a utility program. See Optimization. |
| **Disk Cleanup** | A utility program that deletes unnecessary files from the hard drive, in order to free up storage space. |
| **Disk Error** | Another name for *Check Disk*. |
| **Optimization** | A utility program in *Windows 8.1* which rearranges the data on the hard drive, and regroups or reunites fragmented files. This is also called *Defragmentation*. |
| **Performance Rating Score** | This score indicates the overall performance of your computer, based on the capacity of various computer components. A higher score usually means that the computer performs better and faster than a computer with a lower rating score, especially when advanced tasks are run, where lots of sources are used. No longer available in *Windows 8.1*. |
| **Processor** | The main chip in a computer. The processor (or CPU) performs the greater part of the calculations that make the computer work. |

*- Continue on the next page -*

| **RAM memory** | The main internal storage area used by the computer to run programs and store data. Data is temporarily stored in the RAM-memory, and is lost when the computer is turned off. The RAM memory is also called the internal memory or the working memory. |
| --- | --- |
| **SSD** | Short for *Solid State Drive*. A modern hard drive without any moving parts. It is much faster than the traditional hard drive. |
| **Startup program** | A program that automatically starts up, along with *Windows*. |
| **System info** | Contains advanced, detailed information about the computer's configuration, components, and software, such as drivers. |
| **Uninstall** | To undo the installation of a program, by deleting the program files from the computer. |
| **Windows Experience Index** | This index measures the capabilities of the hardware and software components in your computer and expresses the results in a number, called the performance rating score. No longer available in *Windows 8.1*. |

*Source: Windows Help and Support, Wikipedia*

**Processor**
The processor is the core of your computer. All the operations you do on your computer run through the processor. For example, when you type a text or edit a photo, the processor is busy computing these actions.
Modern processors calculate at breakneck speed. The speed of a processor is measured in *megahertz* or *gigahertz*, for example, 800 MHz or 3 GHz. The higher the number, the faster the processor can compute, and the faster the computer will be.

But in the end, the final speed is also determined by the speed of the other components in your computer. If the processor is fast, but another component is not, congestions will arise, and the computer can slow down. You will notice this, when it becomes harder to open a program and it takes a longer time to save your work.

*- Continue on the next page -*

Throughout the years, a large number of processor types have been developed by various manufacturers. Some well-known types include:

- *Intel 8088/8086/80286*:
  These were the processors used in the first computers. They could process 8 to 16 bits at a time, and that is why they were called 8 or 16-bit processors. One bit signifies one computer signal, for instance, on/off, yes/no, or 0 and 1. Computers can only work with bits. By combining the bits in a row, letters and numbers can be displayed, among other things.
- *Intel 80386/80486*:
  This processor worked with 32 bits at once, which made it faster and able to work with large amounts of data.
- *Intel Pentium/Celeron*:
  A next generation of 32-bit processors, especially suited for *Windows*. A limited number of Celeron processors were also suited for 64-bit applications.
- *Intel Core*:
  The most recent and fastest generation of processors, suited for 32 and 64-bit applications.

Similar types of processors are made by AMD, the other large manufacturing company on the market.

Modern processors are built like multi-core processors. These processors have multiple cores (dual-core has two cores, for example) that can perform independently of one another. This shortens the processing time.
In order to use these processors, both the operating system and the other programs need to make use of the multi-core technology. *Windows* uses this, along with all the current modern programs.

**Memory types**
Besides the hard drives, CDs, and DVDs, the computer uses other types of electronic memory as well. Electronic memory is considerably faster than the mechanical memory of a hard drive, for instance.

RAM          *Random Access Memory*, also called working memory or internal memory. The main internal storage area, used by the computer to run programs and store data. Data is temporarily stored in the RAM memory, and is lost when you turn off or restart the computer.
The RAM memory consists of a number of (cards with) memory chips, and can often be expanded by adding an extra memory card.

*- Continue on the next page -*

Because these chips are very fast, the size of the RAM memory is crucial to the working speed of the computer. Remember that Ram memory comes in various speeds and types. A memory card with the wrong speed may cause problems with the computer.

ROM  *Read Only Memory*, the memory that can only be read. Built-in computer memory that can be read but not modified by a computer. Unlike the RAM memory, the data in the ROM is not deleted when the computer is turned off. Among other things, the ROM memory contains the initial instructions that are necessary for starting up the computer once it is turned on.

Flash  A small device on which data can be stored, such as a USB stick. USB sticks can be connected to the USB ports on a computer. They let you copy data to and from other computers and devices. The information will still be stored in the memory after you have removed the stick from the USB port. A USB stick can be erased and re-used again. Other flash memory types are the cards used in cameras and phones.

Virtual  Temporary storage space on a disk or a USB stick that is used by the computer to run programs that require more RAM memory than available in the computer.

Cache  Cache memory is a very fast but expensive type of memory, built-in in a processor or a hard drive. This memory is used for temporary storage of frequently used data, so that it does not need to be looked up each time. This memory is also often used to save indexing tables that are required to look up data. A large cache memory can considerably increase the speed. Since this type of memory is built into the processor or hard drive, you cannot expand it yourself.

Of all these memory types, the Ram memory has the most influence on the speed while you are working with your computer. But you should keep in mind that the 32-bit version of *Windows* can only use up to 3.5 GB of memory. If the RAM memory is larger, you will gain less speed than you would expect.

**Speeding up your computer with hardware extensions**
Even if you have fine-tuned your computer, the speed will deteriorate eventually. Installing newer, faster hardware may still have some effect. The most effective extensions for a computer are:

*- Continue on the next page -*

| | |
|---|---|
| Faster hard drive | Especially a faster internal hard drive can help you speed up your computer. Make sure to check the disk speed, usually indicated in rpm (rotations per minute). A disk with 5400 rpm is distinctly slower than a disk with 7200 rpm. Apart from this, hard drives are equipped with cache memory, a very fast type of memory that temporarily stores frequently used data, so it does not need to be retrieved from the (slower) hard drive each time you want to use it. Cache memory cannot be expanded, so be sure to choose a large cache memory, if speed is important to you.<br><br>An external hard drive will always experience some delay because of the transfer of data through the USB connection. When you buy an external hard drive, you should also check the speed of its USB connection. If your computer supports USB 3.0, you can use a hard drive with this faster connection.<br><br>The fastest hard drives (internal and external) are of the SSD type. This type has no moving parts, and therefore is very fast. But they are much more expensive than regular hard drives. |
| More RAM memory | RAM memory is very affordable and has great impact on the speed. But keep in mind that the 32-bit version of *Windows* can only use up to a maximum of 3.5 GB. A larger RAM memory will reduce the speed you gain. In the previous *Background Information* section you can read about the different types of memory. |
| Faster graphics card | *Windows* and other programs make ever more use of graphic functions. A faster graphics card will display windows more quickly, and often unburden the processor as well. A graphic card that uses *shared memory* (part of your RAM memory), is significantly slower than a card that has its own graphic memory. |
| Faster processor | This seems the most obvious solution, but it is relatively expensive, and the effect also depends on the rest of your computer. Not every motherboard is suited for faster processors. |

The extension that will give you the most speed depends on the way you use your computer. If you pay attention to the exact moments at which you experience any delays, you may be able to determine which component causes the delay. For example, if this happens while you are playing 3D games, a faster and better graphics (video) card may help to solve the problem.

# 4.10 Tips

 **Tip**

**Windows Performance Index**
It makes a great deal of difference, to which end you use your computer. If you play a lot of 3D games, or do a lot of video editing, you will place much higher demands on your computer than when you only use your computer for browsing the Internet and sending email. The *Windows Performance Index* (*Windows Experience Index*) tells you for which tasks a computer is best suited. The *Windows Performance Index* is only available in *Windows 7*.

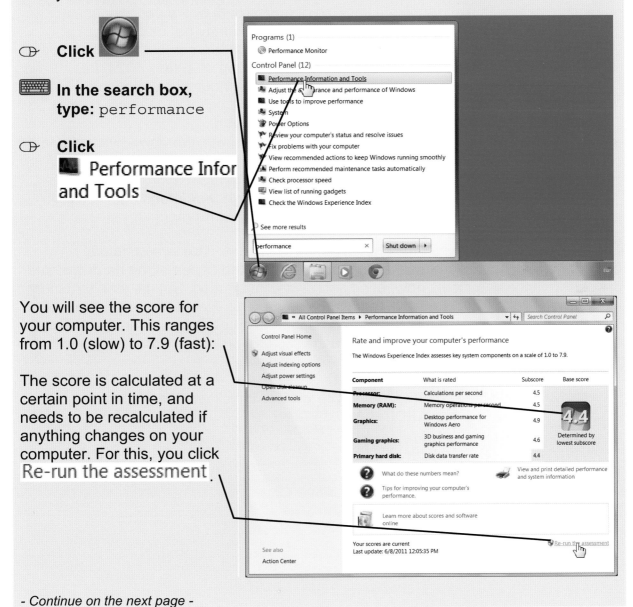

☞ **Click** [Start button]

⌨ **In the search box, type:** `performance`

☞ **Click** [icon] **Performance Infor and Tools**

You will see the score for your computer. This ranges from 1.0 (slow) to 7.9 (fast):

The score is calculated at a certain point in time, and needs to be recalculated if anything changes on your computer. For this, you click **Re-run the assessment**.

*- Continue on the next page -*

The *Windows Performance Index* indicates the overall performance of your system, based on the capacity of the different components in the computer, such as the RAM memory, the processor, hard drive, general graphics performance on the desktop, and graphic display options in 3D.

Here are the general descriptions for the basic scores of this performance index:

- A computer with a score of 1 or 2 is usually capable enough of performing general tasks, such as running daily office applications and searching the Internet. A computer that scores this low is usually not powerful enough to use *Windows* or make use of the advanced multimedia options in *Windows*.
- A computer with a score of 3 is capable of running *Windows Aero* and a large number of *Windows* functions on a basic level. You may not be able to use some of the new, more advanced *Windows* functions. A computer with a score of 3 can display the *Windows* theme with a resolution of 1280 x 1024, for example, but will have trouble displaying the theme on multiple monitors. Another example: this computer will be able to play digital TV, but will have problems displaying HDTV (High Definition Television).
- A computer with a score of 4.0 or 5.0 can run the newer *Windows* functions, and run multiple programs simultaneously.
- A computer with a score of 6.0 or 7.0 has a faster hard drive and supports advanced, heavy-duty graphics applications, such as multi-player games in 3D. It can also handle streaming and recording in HDTV format.

The *Windows Performance Index* has been developed with an eye on future developments in the field of computer technology. As the speed of the hardware and the performance enhances, new rating scores are introduced. But the standards for the individual index levels will still remain the same. This means the basic score of a computer will remain the same, unless you upgrade your computer hardware. For example, if you require a higher performance score in order to work with a specific program, or with *Windows*.

If you have installed new hardware and you want to check whether your score has changed, you can click Re-run the assessment. If you want to display detailed information about the hardware on your computer, you can click

 View and print detailed performance and system information

# Appendices

# Appendix A. How Do I Do That Again?

The actions and exercises in this book are marked with footsteps:
In this appendix you can look up the numbers of the footsteps and read how to execute certain operations.

**1   Close a window**

- Click ❌

**2   Go to the Start screen (only in Windows 8.1)**

- Click 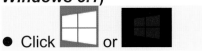 or

*Or:*

- Press

**3   Open the *Control Panel***
*In Windows 8.1, from the Start screen:*
- Type: control panel

- Click

*In Windows 7:*

- Click

- Click Control Panel

**4   Open *Internet Explorer***
*In Windows 8.1 from the taskbar on the desk top:*

- Click

*In Windows 7:*

- Click

- Click All Programs

- Click Internet Explorer

**5   Open *Mozilla Firefox***
*In Windows 8.1, from the Start screen:*
- Type: Mozilla Firefox

- Click Mozilla Firefox

*In Windows 7:*

- Click

- Click All Programs

- Click Mozilla Firefox

**6   Open *Google Chrome***
*In Windows 8.1 from the Start screen:*
- Type: Google Chrome

- Click Google Chrome

*In Windows 7:*

- Click

- Click All Programs

- Click Google Chrome

- Click Google Chrome

$\mathcal{B}$7 **Display the menu bar in**
**Mozilla Firefox**
- Right-click an empty section next to the tab

- Click <u>M</u>enu Bar

$\mathcal{B}$8 **Open *Windows Live Mail***
*In Windows 8.1 from the Start screen:*
- Type: `Windows Live Mail`

- Click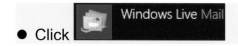

*In Windows 7:*

- Click

- Click All Programs

- Click 🗐 Windows Live Mail

$\mathcal{B}$9 **Open the *Internet options***
**window**
- Click ⚙

- Click Internet options

$\mathcal{B}$10 **Open the *This PC* or *Computer***
**window in *Windows Explorer***
*In both versions, on the taskbar:*
- Click 🖥

*Open This PC in Windows 8.1:*
- Click 🖥 This PC

*Open Computer in Windows 7:*
- Click 🖥 Computer

$\mathcal{B}$11 **Open a website**
- Click the address bar

- Type the web address

- Press

$\mathcal{B}$12 **Open *CCleaner***
*In Windows 8.1, from the Start screen:*
- Type: `CCleaner`

- Click

*In Windows 7:*

- Click 🪟

- Click All Programs

- Click 🗐 CCleaner

- Click 🗐 CCleaner

$\mathcal{B}$13 **Open the *File History* window**
*In Windows 8.1 from the Start screen:*
- Type: `backup`

- Click
  Save backup copies of your files with File History

$\mathcal{B}$14 **Open *Windows Explorer***

- Click 🖥

$\mathcal{B}$15 **Open the *System Properties***
**window**
*In Windows 8.1 from the Start screen:*
- Type: `restore point`

- Click
  Create a restore point

**16 Open the *PC Settings* app**

- Place the pointer in the upper-right corner of the screen

- Move the pointer downwards

- Click

- Click Change PC settings

# Appendix B. Downloading Microsoft Security Essentials

In *Chapter 1 Protecting Your Computer* we have discussed the antivirus program called *Microsoft Security Essentials*. If you have *Windows 7* and you have not yet installed this program to your computer, you can do it like this, through *Internet Explorer*:

☞ **Open** *Internet Explorer* 🐾4

☞ **Open the www.microsoft.com website** 🐾11

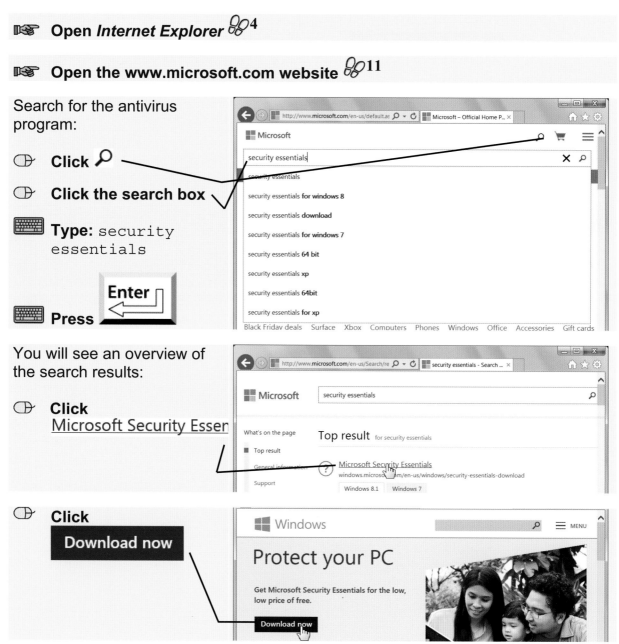

Search for the antivirus program:

🖱 **Click** 🔍

🖱 **Click the search box**

⌨ **Type:** security essentials

⌨ **Press** Enter

You will see an overview of the search results:

🖱 **Click** Microsoft Security Essen...

🖱 **Click** **Download now**

You can install the file right away:

Click **Run**

In *Mozilla Firefox,* you click **Save File** , and after the download operation has finished, you double-click the file. In *Google Chrome*, the download operation will automatically start, and after it has finished, you double-click the file.

When the installation starts, your screen will turn dark. *Windows* will ask for your permission to continue:

☞ **Click** **Yes**

☞ **Close** *Internet Explorer* ⚇¹

You will see the first installation window of *Microsoft Security Essentials*:

At the bottom of the window:

☞ **Click** **Next >**

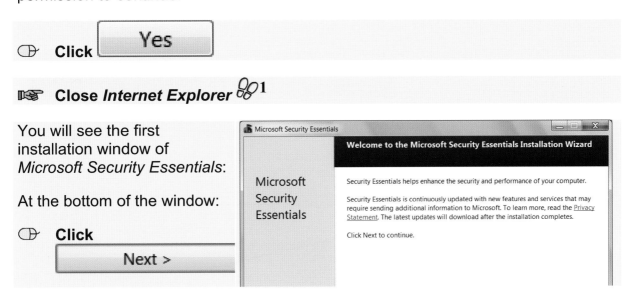

You will need to agree to the user licensing terms:

☞ **Click** **I accept**

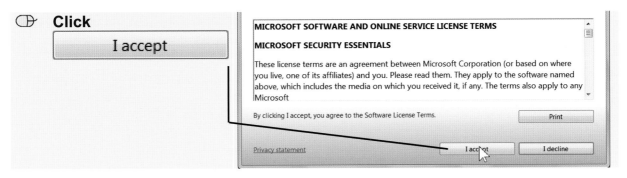

You will be asked for your help in improving the program:

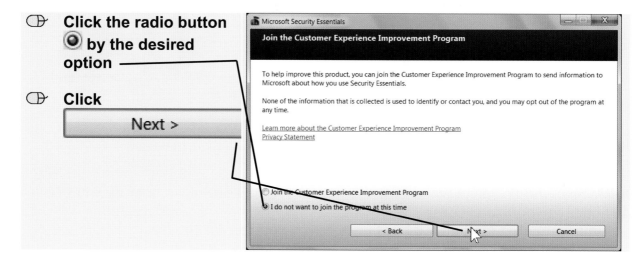

☞ **Click the radio button ◉ by the desired option** ──────

☞ **Click**
> Next >

The program will ask you if you want to enable a firewall as well, if it has not yet been enabled, and if you automatically want to send information on suspect files to *Microsoft*. You are going to allow this:

☞ **Click**
> Next >

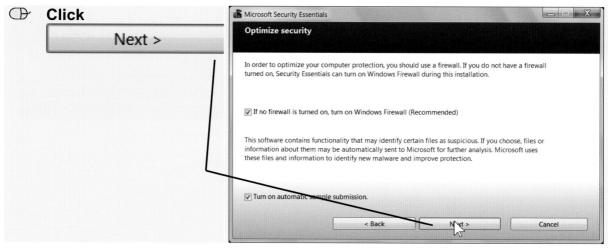

At the bottom of the window:

☞ **Click**
> Install >

At the bottom of the window:

⊕ **Click**

The program installs the most recent definitions for viruses and spyware, and makes sure that everything is updated:

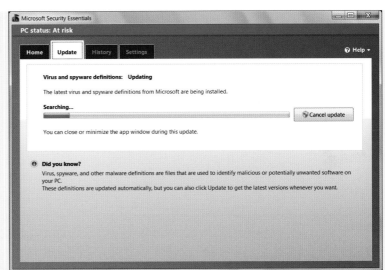

A scan will be started immediately afterwards:

For now, you can cancel this scan.

⊕ **Click**
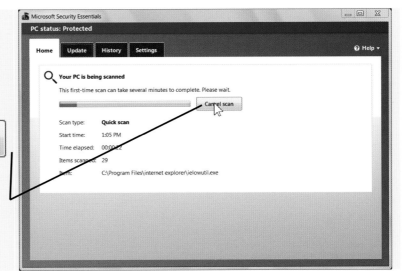

☞ **Continue with *section 1.6 Windows Defender and Microsoft Security Essentials***

# Appendix C. Index

# Word 2013 and 2010 for SENIORS

Microsoft Word is a popular and user-friendly word processing program. This book teaches you the basics of working with documents, from creating and editing documents to formatting text and working with styles and themes. You will also learn some of the

> **LEARN IN YOUR OWN PASE HOW TO WORK WITH WORD**

more advanced features such as working with an index and merging documents. This fully illustrated book features step-by-step instructions that will let you learn Word at your own pace. This is a practical book for the office, school or home!

Please note: In order to work with this book, you need to own Word 2013 or Word 2010 and have it already installed on your computer or have a subscription to Office 365, the online version.

**Author:** Studio Visual Steps
**ISBN** 978 90 5905 110 2
**Book type:** Paperback, full color
**Nr of pages:** 312 pages
**Accompanying website**:
www.visualsteps.com/word2013

*Full color!*

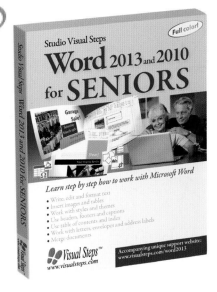

**Learn how to:**
- Write, edit and format text
- Insert images and tables
- Work with styles and themes
- Add headers, footers and captions
- Add a table of contents and an index
- Work with letters, envelopes and address labels
- Merge documents

**Suitable for:**
Microsoft Word 2013 and Word 2010
Windows 8.1, 7 and Vista

**Prior experience:**
Basic computer skills